Reader's Digest

READING skill BUilDER™

ADVANCED

PROJECT EDITOR: **WARREN J. HALLIBURTON**

EDITOR: **LINDA BEECH**

CONSULTANTS:

Jorge Garcia, Ed. D.
Supervisor Secondary Reading
Hillsborough County Public
Schools
Tampa, Florida

Susan Pasquini
Reading Specialist/
English Instructor
Escondido High School
San Diego, California

Frank Vernol
Instructional Learning
Secondary Reading
Dallas Independent School
District
Dallas, Texas

Grace Whittaker
Secondary Reading Supervisor
Boston Public Schools
Boston, Massachusetts

READER'S DIGEST EDUCATIONAL DIVISION
The credits and acknowledgments that appear on the inside
back cover are hereby made a part of this copyright page.
© 1980 by Reader's Digest Services, Inc., Pleasantville, N.Y. 10570. All rights reserved,
including the right to reproduce this book or parts thereof in any form.
Printed in the United States of America.

Reader's Digest ® Trademark Reg. U.S. Pat. Off. Marca Registrada ISBN 0-88300-572-7

□□□ □□□ □ Part 1   Reorder No. B22

silver EdiTion

CONTENTS

   Stories for which Audio Lessons are available.

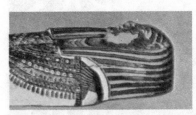

Arun Sadhu

KONDIBA'S DARING DIVE

At first, after the famine had driven him from his village to Bombay, 275 miles (441 kilometers) away, in search of bread, he had tried selling brooms. Though he had little luck peddling his brooms, he soon learned that Bombay is generous to beggars—especially if they are blind. And 25-year-old Kondiba Yeduba Gaikwad had been blind since the age of eight, when he had had smallpox. So, although he hated it, he took to begging.

September 5, 1975, was a typically overcast day in Golibar, a slum northeast of Bombay, India, where Kondiba lived. It was the end of the monsoon season, and the thick cluster of huts was surrounded by mud. Blackish-green water filled the well near Kondiba's home.

The well was important to the people who lived close by. It had been dug two years before because Golibar's only city water tap could not cope with the slum's growing population. There had never been any money for a protective wall around the well, however, and its mouth had gradually widened to 10 feet (3 meters) in diameter as soil and rocks caved in from the sides.

Though the unenclosed well was an invitation to trouble, it had been there for so long that no one worried about it. Three tree trunks had been placed across the hole to support anyone drawing water. A chicken had once fallen in—and been rescued—and that was all. With such a history the well just didn't seem dangerous.

It was noontime, and the men of the colony were away at work. Kondiba had returned to Golibar to eat a little ground meal. His day's begging usually ended when he had five or six rupees (around 65 cents) in a small sack he carried.

Suddenly, there were shouts outside and sounds of great commotion. Kondiba heard a cry: "Someone's fallen into the well!"

Kondiba ran outside and asked to be led to the well.

"Why, what can you do?" he was asked. Still, the blind young beggar was taken to the well. In seconds, Kondiba had pulled off his clothes and jumped into the water. Two teenage boys were already paddling around trying to find a boy who had slipped off one of the tree trunks—slick with moss—while he was pulling up a bucket of water. But the teenagers could not dive.

Although Kondiba had been a good swimmer before he lost his sight, years of malnutrition had sapped his strength. Once, he had been able to dive deep into the wells around his village to pick up shining bits of broken pottery. But it had been many years since he had tried to hold his breath long enough to get to the bottom of such a deep well.

Kondiba floated on the surface for a moment, took a deep breath and dived. Feeling his way along the rocks on the side of the well, he reached the bottom. He felt nothing but soft mud and slimy weeds. With his breath rapidly running out, he had to surface.

It was now two minutes since the boy, Arvind, had fallen in. As Kondiba surfaced without the boy, he could hear people wailing.

The blind man took another deep breath and vanished into the dark waters. His first dive had given him a good idea of the shape of the well, so he went straight down and tried to explore the bottom methodically with his hands. All they felt was a maze of weeds and ooze. There was still no sign of the boy.

Lungs nearly bursting, Kondiba rose once again. Since he had been down longer than the first time, the women and children were getting more and more excited. When he came up, a sigh of disappointment came spontaneously from the growing crowd.

Kondiba's head was above water for just a moment—as he panted heavily and sucked in air—then he dove for the third time. He remembers, in that second, someone shouting, "Can't you find the boy?" Never, in all the years of Kondiba's blindness, had he so missed his sight. If only, only he could see, he might be able to find the drowning boy. He could not know that even normal eyesight would never have helped in that murky water.

By now, three men from another part of the slum had arrived. But they soon admitted that they could not swim. The blind beggar searching below was Arvind's last hope.

Kondiba was already terribly tired, but the well had become an evil thing taunting him. He worked angrily, feeling his way and thinking, "Arvind must be here—he can't have disappeared." Kondiba's ribs were aching and he knew that he couldn't hold his breath much longer.

Just as he was about to twist his body upright and kick himself to the surface, his fingers felt something soft in the weeds. Cloth! He moved his hand farther and touched Arvind's legs. The boy's body was tangled in the mud and weeds.

Kondiba's heart was hammering painfully; he needed to

breathe so badly. But, he re-calls, *I had the boy and had to save him.* Calling on his last reserves of strength, Kondiba felt around for something to grip onto in order to pull Ar-

vind up and out of the net of weeds that trapped him. *A belt!* Clamping his right hand on it, he jerked the boy free, wheeled about, and pushed up. Pain was shooting through his spine

and muscles. His thin body was crying out against the demands being forced upon it.

Maintaining his grip on the boy's belt, Kondiba struggled to move himself upward with his free hand and feet. In his first two dives he had not realized how deep the well was. But now, with his strength going fast and with the additional burden of the boy's weight, he felt as though the crushing load of water would never lift from his heart and lungs.

It seemed forever before he rose the 20 feet (6 meters) from the bottom and broke the surface. Never in his life had he taken such a long and painful trip. While he gasped for breath, hands quickly lifted Arvind up and out of the well. Kondiba held onto the well's slippery, rocky side, his eyes closed.

After Arvind had been hurried away to a hospital, a man helped Kondiba out of the well, a woman patted him on the shoulder, and Kondiba put on his clothes, went home to his half-finished meal and then fell soundly asleep.

The next afternoon, Arvind returned to Golibar. He went at once to Kondiba and touched his feet in gratitude. Kondiba later learned that, had the boy been in the well any longer, his brain would have been damaged from lack of oxygen.

Indeed, Kondiba had saved a life, but his own still had to go on. And for him, that meant begging. By late afternoon, Kondiba was back on the streets of Bombay.

However, word began to travel about the beggar's courage. His picture and the story of the daring rescue were featured in a number of local and national papers. Suddenly, Kondiba was a hero. Congratulations rolled in from high officials, and rewards totaling 12,970 rupees (some $1100) were presented to him.

Today, Kondiba lives in Jalna, a market town close to his native village. He has married and runs a small business. As it happens, Kondiba's brave determination at the well has completely changed his own life. The beggar who hated begging need never beg again.

Number of Words: 1263 ÷ _____ Minutes Reading Time = Rate _____

1. CHARACTERIZATION

Put a check √ before the five words that best describe Kondiba.
Be ready to justify your answers.

_____ **1.** lucky   _____ **6.** self-pitying

_____ **2.** self-centered   _____ **7.** practical

_____ **3.** courageous   _____ **8.** kind

_____ **4.** determined   _____ **9.** humble

_____ **5.** dishonest   _____ **10.** foolish

7 points for each correct answer   SCORE: _____

II. CAUSE/EFFECT

Each of the events in column A caused one of the effects in
column B. Match each cause with the correct effect.

	A		B
_____ **1.**	Kondiba had small-pox as a child.	**a.**	A boy slipped and fell into the well.
_____ **2.**	The tree trunks placed across the well were slick with moss.	**b.**	Kondiba had been blind since the age of eight.
_____ **3.**	Soil and rocks caved in from the sides of the well.	**c.**	Kondiba was able to start a small business.
_____ **4.**	The story of the daring rescue appeared in the papers.	**d.**	The mouth of the well widened to 10 feet in diameter.
_____ **5.**	Rewards totaling $1,100 were given to Kondiba.	**e.**	Suddenly, Kondiba was a hero.

5 points for each correct answer   SCORE: _____

III. SUMMARY

Below are three statements from the selection. Put a check √ before the one that gives the best summary of the article.

_____ **1.** Never, in all the years of Kondiba's blindness, had he so missed his sight.

_____ **2.** As it happens, Kondiba's brave determination at the well has completely changed his own life.

_____ **3.** Indeed, Kondiba had saved a life, but his own had to go on.

20 points for correct answer   SCORE: _____

IV. SKIMMING

Skim through the selection to find the answer to each of the following questions. (Write the answers in the blanks.)

1. How old was Kondiba when the story began? _____

2. What was the name of the slum where Kondiba lived?

   _____

3. How did he try to make a living before turning to begging?

   _____

4. Where did Kondiba go to beg every day? _____

5 points for each correct answer   SCORE: _____

PERFECT TOTAL SCORE: 100   TOTAL SCORE: _____

V. QUESTIONS FOR THOUGHT

What motivated Kondiba to jump into the well after the boy? How might you have reacted to such an accident? Explain.

EVELYN FIORE

HOW TO BE YOUR OWN FAMILY HISTORIAN

Not so long ago family histories remained in family scrapbooks, Bibles, or trunks. Today, family research is one of the country's most popular hobbies. Thousands of ordinary people are following the example of Alex Haley, author of *Roots*. Haley's painstaking tracking of his family's path back to the shores of the Gambia River in Africa struck real fire in people's interest in the past. Revealing the great drama found in just one unknown, unrecorded family line, he reminded people that no matter who they are, they've all got masses of ancestors behind them, human beings who lived, worked, suffered, failed, or succeeded.

Chances are that if one had as an ancestor a King Edward the Confessor,* or even an Attila the Hun, he would already know about it. Most folks will not hit such historical pay dirt. But history isn't just written in capital letters. Some family members will have lived through the great events of their times—the Great Depression, the potato famine, the westward push of Lewis and Clark. The important thing is that people connect themselves via their blood lines to some life in the past. As Haley's grandmother, Kizzy, said in *Roots*, "We strong because we know where we come from."

How *do* you set out to find your great-grandparents, and, with luck, all the fascinating people who came before them? One expert suggests that you first get what you already know out of your head and onto paper, in the form of a family tree. Start with information you already have or that is easily available, because you want experience be-

* A king of England from A.D. 1002 to A.D. 1066.

An African *griot* (story teller) recounting an historical event to children in a village

fore you really start digging.

Many books on genealogy will include family-tree diagrams. Preprinted sheets can also be purchased at some bookstores. For a full-featured history you need something big, like posterboard or brown wrapping paper. This is what Rockefeller family historians have used. On a large-scale tree you'll want to include places and time of births, marriages, and deaths. You might also want to record places of residence, schooling, occupation, hobbies, religious ties and any remembered accomplishments or characteristics that will later be helpful when you try to flesh out the person behind the facts.

Then, starting with living relatives, the oldest ones first, you become detective, reporter and historian. In other words, start asking questions. The idea is to end up with useful interviews, not just chummy chats.

A portable tape recorder

with a built-in microphone is helpful for these talks. The tapes themselves become invaluable records of people your own children may never get a chance to meet. The individual's personality comes across in voice tone, speech pattern, use of language, all sorts of details that are

Armed with a tape recorder, a young girl is prepared to make the most of her interview.

difficult to get down on paper.

In *Roots*, Haley tells about the *griots* of Africa, storytellers who preserve the history of their people through oral language. Let the people you talk to know they are modern-day *griots*. Their tales carry forward the events of the past.

Some questions you might start with to warm up your *griots* are:

1. What do you know about the original family surname?

2. What stories have come down to you—about parents, grandparents, other relations?

3. What do you know about their childhoods, schooling, marriages, work, activities?

4. Is there a notorious character in the family's past?

5. How did your ancestors meet and marry? Are there any unusual love stories in anyone's memory?

6. Have any historical events (wars, floods, etc.) particularly affected the family?

7. Are there stories about fortunes made, almost made, lost?

8. Is there a family cemetery or plot?

9. If all else fails, start with a forward: "What's the earliest thing you remember?" This question creates a starting point.

Keep in mind that you're after significant facts—where folks came from, how they lived, what was happening around them at the time, and so on. A great finishing ploy—remember, you're dealing with relatives!—is to tell Aunt Sophie as you close your talk with her that the next person you're going to see is Uncle Harry. With luck, her eyes will light up and she'll say "Oh, *him*!" and give a half-hour of background on Uncle Harry. This is especially handy if you've never met Uncle Harry.

Remember that in each interview you're after more than words. Look for family papers: photographs, diaries, postcards from long-forgotten holidays, old newspaper clippings, letters, even old school notebooks or texts.

After each interview, file your tapes and any other material you've gotten (carefully marked with name, place of interview and date). Now you're ready for the next step—paper work. This means reading documents, tracking down records, or spending hours over a census report.

First, be sure you know which family line you want to follow. At the grandparent level there are already four possibilities. The most favorite choice, of course, is to track the name you bear.

If you have traced someone back to an American town, go there if you can. If that's not practical, write. Start with the librarian of the town. This will apply whether you're on the spot or working by mail. Even small-town libraries may come up with rich files of regional lore: diaries, journals, old county maps naming landholders, histories of local families, commercial or agricultural developments that might have touched your family.

Libraries can also help you contact local, state, or regional historical societies. Their collections can contain masses of material important to the area—and maybe to you. If you think them helpful, there are also centers in which to check wartime records, right back to the Revolution.

If you are able to actually visit the town, remember to consult basic files of local newspapers. Also, investigate any unions, workmen's circles or other organizations that might have information.

You cannot talk to neighbors, visit an old churchyard, or pick up a surprising bit of ancient gossip unless you do go "back home" in person. However, you can write to the National Archives in Washington, D.C. (See page 21.) Experts at the National Archives can be helpful when it comes to problems, such as trying to sift information out of immigration records or shipping manifests.

If you're going to check immigration records, you will have to write to the Department of Immigration. Before you do that, try to find out the place at which your immigrant relative came into the country, the place from which he or she came, and if possible be sure of the name under which this person entered the country. Complicated Middle European names were often shortened by clerks too busy to get all the syllables down. Many were simplified later by the newcomers themselves, who found their long names burdensome in the new society. The Department of Immigration can be helpful, but only if you give them some help to start with. (See chart on page 21 for address.)

Almost any American (always excepting the American Indian) will sooner or later come to the water's edge. You may go back to the 1600s before you hit this point, or only to the

mass immigrations of the last 150 years. But let your search get a real grip on you; it is certain to take you (in writing) across one of the oceans.

There are helpful private organizations here in the United States. One resource center not to be overlooked is the Mormon Genealogical Society in Salt Lake City, Utah. In the Mormon faith, family research is not a hobby but a requirement. Over many years the Salt Lake City society has built up a library, unique in size and scope, of microfilmed source materials from all over the world. Its massive collection of vital facts, land, probate, legal, church and other records is not confined to church members, but is universal. You do not have to be a church member to use it. Anyone who writes to the society is welcome to any help the library can provide. Copies of records are available for a small fee.

There is no one right way to set up a family-history project. In many cases several family members have gotten involved in the search. "The shared enthusiasm of parents, grandparents, and students can be incredible," reports one school principal who set up a Family Heritage Program. In a neighborhood where ethnic hostility was a life-style, students not only got back into communication with their own families but began to talk meaningfully with one another. They developed close bonds as they pursued probably the first common goals they had ever shared together.

On a personal scale, the rewards of a search become clear even as you start. You find a more intimate meaning in history. Your ethnic ties come alive, and a faraway part of the world may suddenly leap into focus before your very eyes.

But chiefly, the search rewards you with a framework and roots of your own—with a sense of belonging. As you prepare, for yourself and those who come after you, the story of those who came before, you are fitting yourself into the stream of time. In the words of anthropologist Margaret Mead, this is "a way of binding together the past, the present, and the future of us all."

HOW TO BEGIN YOUR GENEALOGICAL SEARCH

The most useful books to begin with:

Searching for Your Ancestors by Gilbert H. Doane (Bantam Books). A classic do-it-yourself manual

The Genealogist's Encyclopedia by L. G. Pine (Weybright and Talley). Valuable documentation of European sources

Family History for Fun and Profit by Vincent L. Jones, Arlene H. Eagle and Mildred H. Christensen (The Genealogical Institute, Salt Lake City, Utah). A primer on procedure and record keeping

Good sources to visit or write to:

National Archives, Genealogical Division, 8th and Pennsylvania N.W., Washington D.C. 20408 (from whom you can also get the addresses of Archives branches across the country)

Library of Congress, Genealogical Division, 10 1st Street S.E., Washington, D.C. 20540

Library, Daughters of the American Revolution, 1776 D Street N.W. Washington, D.C. 20006

Department of Immigration, Washington, D.C. (or the nearest regional office)

For Jewish research: YIVO Center for Advanced Jewish Studies, 1048 Fifth Ave., New York, N.Y. 10028

For Black research: Schomburg Center for Research in Black Culture, 103 West 135th St., New York, N.Y. 10030

The Genealogical Helper, Everton Publishers, Logan, Utah, will accept announcements of family research projects

Number of Words: 1736 ÷ _____ Minutes Reading Time = Rate _____

I. CLASSIFYING

Based on the selection, put each statement below into one of the following categories: (Write a, b or c in the blank.)

    a. REASONS FOR RESEARCHING YOUR FAMILY HISTORY
    b. METHODS OF RESEARCHING YOUR FAMILY HISTORY
    c. REWARDS OF RESEARCHING YOUR FAMILY HISTORY

_____ **1.** Remember to consult basic files of local newspapers.

_____ **2.** Most people hope to uncover some great drama in their family line.

_____ **3.** Your ethnic ties come alive, and a faraway part of the world may suddenly leap into focus.

_____ **4.** The important thing is that people want to learn about their past family lines.

_____ **5.** You find that you are fitting into the stream of time.

6 points for each correct answer   SCORE: _____

II. GENERALIZATIONS

Based on the information in this selection, certain generalizations may be made. Put a check ✓ before each of three sentences below that makes a generalization.

_____ **1.** Most people will not find a world-famous figure in their family line.

_____ **2.** For most people, the search will take them in writing across one of the oceans.

_____ **3.** In other words, you start asking questions.

_____ **4.** Most schools are starting Family Heritage Programs.

_____ **5.** Alex Haley has been an inspiration to all Americans.

10 points for each correct answer   SCORE: _____

III. OUTLINING

Complete the outline below by copying each of the following sentences in its proper place.

 1. Include all known facts about each person.
 2. Write to library in that town.
 3. Check wartime records.
 4. Interview your relatives.

 I. Start with information you already have.
   A. Make a family-tree diagram.

   B. _____

 II. _____
   A. Ask pertinent questions.
   B. Use a tape recorder.
   C. Ask for any family documents.
 III. Do paperwork.
   A. Decide which family line you want to follow.
     1. Go to person's hometown, if possible.

     2. _____

   B. Track down sources of information.
     1. Visit historical societies.

     2. _____

     3. Research newspaper files.
     4. Visit national archives.
     5. Contact Department of Immigration.

10 points for each correct answer   SCORE: _____

PERFECT TOTAL SCORE: 100   TOTAL SCORE: _____

IV. QUESTION FOR THOUGHT

In what ways can an understanding of the past help you develop an outlook for the future?

Erma Bombeck

IF LiFE IS a BOWL

OF CHeRRieS....

I've always worried a lot, and frankly I'm good at it. I worry about a snake coming up through the kitchen drain, and about the world ending and me stuck with three hours on a 24-hour cold pill. I worry about scientists discovering that lettuce has been fat-tening all along, or about what the dog will think when he sees me getting out of the shower. But these days I worry most about the family—about its sur-vival in a world that changes almost daily.

To my way of thinking, fore-most of the problems that rip

the family apart is the latest math method. Before this method, I had a mysterious air about me. I never said anything, but my children were sure that I had invented fire. Then we began to have "input" with one another, and one day my daughter said, "Mom, what's a variable?"

"Where did you read that word?"

"It's in my math book," she said. "I was hoping you could help me." She went to her room, locked her door and I never saw her again until after she graduated.

And what modern-day mother isn't intimidated when she has a problem like this? I don't think there's anything that makes my morning like a kid looking up from his cereal and saying casually, "I have to have a note saying I was sick or my teacher won't let me back into school."

"I suppose it has to be written on paper," I asked, slumping miserably over the table.

"The one you wrote on waxed paper she couldn't read. But if you can't find paper, I could stay home for another day or two."

I tore a piece of wallpaper off the wall and said, "Get a pencil." After a 15-minute

search, we finally found a stub in the lint trap of the washing machine.

"Dear Mrs. Weems," I wrote. "Please excuse Brucie's absence from school yesterday. He had an upset stomach and. . . ."

"Cross out upset stomach," he ordered. "The last time you wrote that she put me next to the door and didn't take her eyes off me all day."

My kids always talk a lot about ecology. Yet they harbor the No. 1 pollutant in the country: gym clothes. A pair of shorts, a shirt and a pair of gym shoes walked into the laundry room under their own steam last Wednesday and leaned helplessly against the wall. As I stood there watching, a potted plant withered and died before my eyes.

Blinking back the tears, I yelled to my son, "How long has it been since these clothes have been washed?"

"Since the beginning of the school year," he shouted back.

"What school year?"

"Last year."

There are other aspects about kids which confuse me. For example: Who is "I. Dunno?"

Ever since I can remember,

our home has had a fourth child—I. Dunno. Everyone sees him but me. All I know is that he's rotten.

Who left the front door open?

I. Dunno.

Who let the soap melt down the drain?

I. Dunno.

Frankly, I. Dunno is driving me wild. He's lost two umbrellas, four pairs of boots and a bicycle. Once, he left a thermos of milk in the car for three whole weeks.

This morning at breakfast I asked, "Who wants liver for dinner this evening?"

The reply: "I don't care."

That can only mean one thing. I. Dunno has a brother.

I have never understood how it is that a kid can climb up on the roof, scale the TV antenna and rescue the cat, yet cannot walk down the hall without grabbing both walls with grub-

by hands, for balance. Or how it is that a small child can kiss the dog on the lips, chew gum that he found in the ashtray and put his mouth over a muddy garden hose, yet refuse to drink from a glass—"yech!"—because his brother has just used it.

Then there are the car incidents. My eldest took her car to the garage for repairs last week and used my car while hers was being fixed. The day her car came back, she returned my keys and said, "Hey, Mum, you owe me three dollars for the gas I put in your car."

I could not believe it.

Then I remembered a letter a teenager had written me after she had read one of my books. Maybe that would get through to my daughter.

"Listen to this," I said, reading from the letter. "Parents go through life saying to their children, 'I've worked my fingers to the bone for you, and what do I get in return?'

"You want an answer, Mrs. Bombeck? You get messy rooms, messy hair, dirty fingernails, raided refrigerators. You get something else, too. You get someone who loves you, but

never takes the time to tell you in words. You get someone who'll defend you at every turn even though you do wear orthopedic socks and clean clothes every day.

"And when we leave home, there will be a little tug at our hearts because we know we will miss you, and home, and everything it meant. But most of all, we will miss the constant assurances of how very much you love us."

Her eyes misty, my daughter looked up. "Does that mean I don't get the three dollars?" she asked me.

When you're an orthodox worrier, as I am, some days are worse than others. But not even a professional pessimist would believe what I went through last week.

It began on Monday morning when the kids filed into the kitchen completely dressed. I asked, "Who wants something ironed before school?" No one spoke! Then my car with the new battery actually started. I found a parking place in front of the supermarket and got a shopping cart with four wheels that all went in the same direction at the same time.

All of this made me feel edgy, but I figured things would soon get back to normal. They didn't.

By Thursday I was a wreck anticipating what was in store for me; but it didn't happen. I ran for a bus and caught it. The lady who sells cosmetics door to door refused me service, saying I already looked terrific. The check book balanced.

On Friday, I was sobbing into a dish towel when my husband tried to comfort me. "I can't help it," I said. "Things were never meant to go this well. I'm worried."

"Now, now," he said, patting my shoulder. "Things can't go rotten all the time."

"But this isn't like us," I whined. "Bad times I can handle. It's the good times that drive me crazy. When is the other shoe going to drop?"

Just then we heard a car turn into the garage, followed by the sickening scrape of a tender fender meeting an immovable wall. We looked at each other and smiled.

Things were looking up.

Number of Words: 1164 ÷ _____ Minutes Reading Time = Rate _____

I. STORY ELEMENTS

The sentences below describe styles used by the writer. Complete each sentence by placing a check √ in front of the best ending for it.

1. The mood of this story is
   _____ **a.** bitter.
   _____ **b.** humorous.
   _____ **c.** critical.
2. The story could best be described as
   _____ **a.** light reading matter.
   _____ **b.** food for thought.
   _____ **c.** an emotional experience.
3. The mood of the story is achieved by
   _____ **a.** quoting many research sources.
   _____ **b.** writing about people who never existed.
   _____ **c.** describing ridiculous situations as though they were real.

10 points for each correct answer   SCORE:_____

II. LANGUAGE USAGE

The following sentences introduce expressions used in the selection. Write the letter that defines the italicized words.

_____ 1. When a kid *scales* a TV antenna, he or she
   a. draws a picture of it.
   b. makes a model of it.
   c. climbs up on it.

_____ 2. When people *file* into a room, they usually
   a. enter together.   **b.** enter one at a time.
   c. fill the room.

_____ 3. When things are *looking up*, they are
   a. unbearable.   **b.** improving.   **c.** unexplainable.

_____ **4.** When you want to *get through* to a person, you are trying to make that person
  a. understand something.   **b.** hear something.
  c. do something.

_____ **5.** Feeling a *little tug at one's heart* usually shows
  a. sadness.   **b.** a heart attack.   **c.** anger.

8 points for each correct answer   SCORE:_____

III. AUTHOR'S PURPOSE

Write the letter of the ending that best completes each statement.

_____ **1.** The selection consists of
  a. a series of little stories.
  b. a list of statistics.
  c. summaries of interviews with people.

_____ **2.** The author's style of writing consists of
  a. a dull retelling of facts.
  b. quoting other writers.
  c. exaggerating everyday situations.

_____ **3.** The author makes the most ordinary events seem
  a. complicated.
  b. mysterious.
  c. funny.

10 points for each correct answer   SCORE:_____

PERFECT TOTAL SCORE: 100   TOTAL SCORE:_____

IV. QUESTIONS FOR THOUGHT

Did you find this selection funny or not? If so, what was it that entertained you? Or, why didn't you find this selection funny?

Al Stark

DEADLY HOT PEPPERS

Diane Sprenger, a nurse at St. Joseph's Mercy Hospital in Pontiac, Michigan, was on duty the night of March 29. Toward the end of her shift, she noticed that the lights in the hospital corridors bothered her. After work she went home and, before going to bed, ate some cheese. She had trouble swallowing, but thought she was just tired.

Next morning Diane knew she was sick. She could hardly talk. She felt dizzy and couldn't focus her eyes.

Diane made a noon appointment with a doctor. He checked her over and thought she might be suffering from hysteria. (Recent news about her father's health had come as a terrible blow.) So the doctor gave Diane some medicine and sent her home. She made herself a cup of hot chocolate, but couldn't swallow it. Instead, she went into a choking fit. When it was over, she asked her mother to drive her to St. Joseph's Hospital.

When a neurosurgeon examined Diane, her face was paralyzed, she was drooling and had double vision. He admitted Diane to the hospital, where she would be under close observation, and where another doctor, Lionel Glass, would look at her.

During the night, Diane got worse. Dr. Glass found her quite sick. She had difficulty breathing. And she looked bad, very bad. When she tried to swallow, she felt as if there were a golf ball in her throat. It was acute bulbar paralysis.

Because of her breathing problems, Dr. Glass had Diane moved to intensive care. There she was hooked up to a respirator, and two specialists were called in to keep her alive while Dr. Glass tried to figure out what was killing her.

Tests were taken, including a spinal tap: no sign of anything. In time, almost every possible cause was crossed out except botulism. This is a food poisoning caused by bacteria that grow in improperly preserved food. Botulism kills about 20 percent of those who get it.

Says Dr. Glass, "I can't remember when I first said the frightening word out loud. But I had it in mind as my first guess. Another doctor asked, 'What do you think?' and I said, 'Botulism first.'"

Something happened that made Dr. Glass' guess look better. "A resident stepped up," he recalls, "and asked if I could come to the emergency room to look at a curious case. I asked what the symptoms were, and he told me difficulty in swallowing, difficulty with vision, difficulty with speech, difficulty with breathing—everything Diane Sprenger had.

"We ran down to emergency and there lay John Slater." Slater, a 26-year-old deacon at St. Hugo of the Hills Catholic Church in Bloomfield Hills, had become ill and had gone to his physician only a few hours before.

This was a big break in the case. It would be very rare for a hospital to admit two victims of something like polio within hours of each other. But botulism almost always affects more than one person, since the poisoned food is usually eaten by several people.

As soon as Dr. Glass had examined Slater, he called the State Health Department to ask if botulism had appeared anywhere in the state recently. This was at 3 p.m. on Thursday, March 31.

By 4 p.m., health worker Mel Goldman and a public-health nurse were at St. Joseph's questioning the patients' friends and relatives.

The Center for Disease Control in Atlanta, Georgia, is the nation's clearinghouse and command post in epidemics. Its man in Michigan was sent to St. Joseph's with three bottles of botulism antitoxin. Meanwhile, health officials began lining up more antitoxin from across the nation. No one knew yet how many people might be involved, but already doctors were fearful that the outbreak could get very big and might be difficult to control.

In the intensive-care unit,

Mel Goldman was hoping for a lead. Botulism, he knew, is almost always caused by food that has been improperly canned at home. Diane Sprenger and John Slater didn't know each other. This suggested they had been poisoned in a public restaurant. But which one? And how many more people might be poisoned if it weren't found quickly and closed down?

The best Diane could do by now was nod or shake her head. Questioning a member of the staff, Goldman learned about a pizza ordered by a patient, which she and Diane had shared on Tuesday night. He also believed that on Monday night after work, Diane had eaten a mini-nacho (peppers and cheese on corn chips) at Trini and Carmen's, a Mexican restaurant near the hospital.

Goldman went to the phone to call in his information. A nurse overheard him. She didn't feel well, and her symptoms were similar to those Goldman was describing. She told him so and also said she had eaten out only once that week—at Trini and Carmen's.

Slater, lying nearby, overheard some of this. He couldn't speak, but was able to ring for a nurse. "Were you talking about nachos?" he wrote on a pad. "I had nachos, too."

Health officials rushed to Trini and Carmen's. In a kitchen closet they found a jar of home-canned peppers. It had been opened. On the busy night of March 28, the cook, thinking she had run out of fresh peppers, had grabbed the jar and used the peppers in it to prepare hot sauce for the popular Mexican food.

At 8:30 p.m., on Thursday, an order came to close down food service in the restaurant. During the period when the nachos were served, the restaurant had had some 400 customers.

By now, botulism victims were beginning to stream into emergency rooms at hospitals throughout the area. When the antitoxin arrived, it was given to Diane Sprenger and John Slater, who were among the most seriously ill. But the terrible questions remained:

How many more people were poisoned? And how could they be warned so they would seek early help?

The decision to make an announcement was reached after 11 p.m. The first announcement was made on television at about 11:45 p.m.

Soon, St. Joseph's was flooded with calls. So was Crittenton Hospital, nearby. Crittenton's emergency room became so crowded, there were not enough doctors to talk to all the people. At least ten persons were admitted to St. Joseph's and Crittenton with botulism that night, and the phones kept ringing.

The number of cases continued to climb on Friday. Customers of Trini and Carmen's showed up in hospitals for miles around.

Jars of peppers from the restaurant had been sent to the labs in Atlanta. On Saturday, April 2, the report came back: some peppers contained the botulism poison. So did samples taken from the first patients. The source of the poisoning was now confirmed.

That same day, word came from doctors at Little Traverse Hospital in Petoskey, Mich., 260 miles (418 kilometers) to the northwest. Two hospital employees who had been to Pontiac and had eaten at Trini and Carmen's Restaurant had been admitted there.

The last new case came to light on Wednesday, April 7. The next day it was announced that the trouble was over. Botulism may show itself in a person up to eight days after eating the poisoned food. The eight days had now passed.

Happily, no one died. Through luck, fast action, medicine and quick detective work, death was held off. It had been the biggest single outbreak of botulism in U.S. history: the number of victims was near 50. Yet every one of those people lived.

In time the most seriously ill got better. By April 14, John Slater was recovering at his mother's home in Dearborn, very hoarse and weak but getting stronger. Both John and Diane are now fully recovered.

Number of Words: 1304 ÷ _____ Minutes Reading Time = Rate _____

I. CAUSE/EFFECT

The numbered sentences tell what caused something to happen. Circle the letter (a, b or c) of the sentence below that tells about this effect.

1. Diane Sprenger ate poisoned food.
   a. She couldn't breathe.
   b. She worked the night shift.
   c. She immediately rushed to the hospital.
2. A cook at Trini and Carmen's thought she had run out of fresh peppers.
   a. She ordered another bushelful.
   b. She used some homemade peppers in a jar.
   c. She discovered her mistake.
3. A warning about botulism was made on TV.
   a. The disease spread.
   b. People with botulism symptoms rushed to hospitals.
   c. Antitoxin was given to Diane.

---

10 points for each correct answer   SCORE:_____

II. SKIMMING

Read each question carefully. Then go back and skim the article. Draw a circle around the letter (a, b or c) of the correct answer.

1. Which of the following is *not* a symptom of botulism?
   a. blurred vision   **b.** difficulty in swallowing
   c. bleeding
2. What is the death rate of botulism victims?
   a. 20 percent   **b.** 50 percent   **c.** 35 percent
3. Where is the Center for Disease Control?
   a. Pontiac, Michigan   b. Atlanta, Georgia
   c. Washington, D.C.
4. Up to how long can it take for botulism to show itself in a victim?
   a. 8 days   **b.** 15 days   **c.** 3 days

5. How many victims were in this particular outbreak?
   a. 25   **b.** 50   **c.** 150

8 points for each correct answer   SCORE:_____

III. PROBLEM SOLVING

Six of the facts below helped doctors solve the mystery of Diane's strange illness. Put a check √ before each of the six.

_____ **1.** Diane Sprenger was a nurse.
_____ **2.** John Slater was admitted to the emergency room with the same symptoms as Diane.
_____ **3.** Diane and John didn't know each other, suggesting that they had been poisoned in a public restaurant.
_____ **4.** Health official Mel Goldman questioned Diane about where she had eaten that week.
_____ **5.** Diane had eaten a mini-nacho at a nearby Mexican restaurant.
_____ **6.** Slater and another nurse with similar symptoms had eaten nachos at the same restaurant.
_____ **7.** The Center for Disease Control sent three bottles of botulism antitoxin.
_____ **8.** An opened jar of home-canned peppers found at Trini and Carmen's proved to contain botulism.
_____ **9.** The antitoxin was given to Diane and John.
_____ **10.** Diane is now back to work.

5 points for each correct answer   SCORE:_____

PERFECT TOTAL SCORE: 100   TOTAL SCORE:_____

IV. QUESTION FOR THOUGHT

How did "luck, fast action, medicine and quick detective work" help save the lives of the botulism victims? Explain each one.

James Gaines

FEAR AND MAGIC
FOR ANDRÉ WATTS

André Watts sits alone in a small music room at the Huntington, Long Island, high school, playing on an out-of-tune piano. The passage is from Schubert's *B-flat Impromptu.* Any child who has taken piano lessons can play it; yet for a concert pianist its very simplicity can be nerve-racking, particularly as the first piece of a program. It is an invitation to big mistakes.

Watts makes one slip on this old, brassy piano. Upset, he slides quickly off the bench and begins to pace up and down. There is a knock on the door, and Watts greets a friend. As they talk, Watts grows calm. But then his face suddenly darkens, and his eyes find something worrisome in the middle distance. "Man," he says with a rush of breath, "these small-town concerts really get to me—worse than New York."

Why the fear? One of the most widely known pianists in the country, Watts has been on the stage for 15 years. Stage fright could explain some of his unease. But Watts is best known for the great show-pieces of concerts. The kind of pieces audiences respond to— no matter who is playing. The project offers none of that se-curity. He is setting out on an all-Schubert series (42 concerts in 22 U.S. cities) in honor of the anniversary of the composer's death.

In at least one sense, Schubert—who died all but penni-less at 31—will serve him well. "My manager said to me this morning, 'André, do you real-ize you'll make more money on this series than Schubert made in his whole lifetime?' " Watts, who was born in 1946, earns well into six figures per year. On this night, the music of Schubert seems to be making Watts nervous. "If, right before you play a passage, you think it's not going to work, it's not," he says. "You can stake your life on it."

After what Watts calls his "pre-puffs on a cigar," absent-mindedly touching the keys of the piano, rubbing some tonic in his hair and fixing his white tie—he walks alone through a darkened school hall to the wings of the stage.

An only child, Watts was born in Nuremberg, Germany, in 1946 to a black American soldier and his Hungarian war bride. When André was 8, the family moved to Philadelphia.

His mother gave André his first piano lesson in Germany

at 6; and in the United States he went to the Philadelphia Musical Academy. When he was 9, he was chosen from among 40 contestants to play with the Philadelphia Orchestra in a young people's concert. A year later he played with them again. He practiced every day; and when he tried to avoid it, his mother would tell him about the careers of famous musicians, most often Liszt's. If that failed to make him want to practice, the unimpressed André would get a slap.

At about the age of 14, André developed what he calls a "healthy fanaticism" for playing the piano.

By the time he was 16 he had won all the local contests. That year he heard that Leonard Bernstein, the famous orchestra conductor, was holding auditions in New York City, and rushed to apply. Bernstein himself says he "flipped" over André's playing.

Not long after that, another musician canceled a concert with the Philharmonic, and Bernstein called on Watts. New York was in the middle of a newspaper strike at the time, and the change was not announced publicly.

The audience was noisily displeased when a skinny kid walked onstage. But by the end of his playing, the entire audience jumped to its feet and cheered. Even the members of the orchestra stood up and clapped. Watts went offstage in a daze. "It was very strange," he says. "It took a while to really figure out what had happened."

Invitations to play began piling up. Mrs. Watts, however,

André Watts receiving congratulations for his successful concert debut with New York Philharmonic from Leonard Bernstein

was determined to see her son through high school and through the new pieces he would have to master for a career. Watts finished the 11th and 12th grades in the next eight months and played only six concerts. The next year he played 12, the next 15, and soon he was up to his present average of 100. He also began taking classes toward the artist's diploma he won at Baltimore's Peabody Conservatory in 1972. There he studied with the famous pianist and conductor Leon Fleisher, who was "my only real teacher."

Watts lives in New York City and, at least five weeks a year, in a 6-acre (2-hectare) spread in upstate New York. The phone rings less often there, and he enjoys the chores and lawn sports of the country.

Mrs. Watts, who once went everywhere with him, now stays mostly in New York. "People didn't understand our closeness," he says of talk that he was a "stage mother's" boy. "She is, after all, the closest relative I have; and it's really quite true that, when you're in the public eye, you have few friends and lots of acquaintances. People start lying to you, giving you compliments you don't deserve. So you have

to develop just the right kind of self-centeredness, observe yourself, watch where you're going."

Watts believes that to direct a strong force into his music is what the pianist's gift is all about. "On recordings, the audience doesn't feel your presence," he explains. "But in the hall you can bring off your interpretation by force of will. Music must speak to the emotions. It must make a conversation—like I say something to you, and then I qualify it in another tone of voice. That's exactly what the musical line is. Playing Schubert is like walking down the street with a pushcart full of beautiful melodies, holding them out saying, 'Won't you have one? Don't you love this one?' You have to be able to put the music on a platter and wave that platter under the nose of every person in the hall."

Watts believes in his ability to do that, but cannot quite believe in too much praise. "You know that your work will never be finished and you'll never give everything you have. There's a kind of pleasure in that pain, but even when you're having a big success— you know, people having heart attacks in the hall—you go home and ask yourself what it would've been like if you'd used *all* your abilities."

What separates brilliance from competence? It is the basic question all performers ask themselves, and one that Watts isn't eager to discuss. "It takes hard work to bring the music out," he says. "It would be too easy for me to mystify the process." He makes his own job sound commonplace. And yet Watts has "a desire," he admits, "to do the impossible." He is fascinated by Harry Houdini and takes great pleasure in talking about the secrets of the magician's acts. "Magic is all explainable, you see!" he exclaims. "What Houdini had was guts—that is the name of the game. I really believe that all people are born with that ability—to live life creatively, to the hilt. But from the moment the doctor slaps your bottom, it begins to get squelched. Fear is the big thing. People are just afraid. I don't blame them for feeling this way either."

And is that what he means when he talks about not playing carefully—not giving in to fear? "Look," he says, his voice going low, "the ideal musical performer is two people; meaning, I sit at the piano and I'm really all there, you know, intending every note. But at the same time there's another me at my shoulder, saying, 'You're going too fast. Pull it back.'

"And that's something you have to work on. Total involvement is no good; total uninvolvement is no good; both are necessary. And there's nothing easy about that. It's a funny business. When you start to talk about performing, I think you can get very scared."

Watts marches onstage, and his black hair turns sun-yellow in the light. At the piano, he puts a hand on the music rack, bows to the audience, then sits down and adjusts the bench slightly. His elbows go up, and his fingers touch the keys lightly. It's a noisy audience, he says to himself, and starts to tune them out.

The music begins, and an unnameable feeling in his stomach begins to grow. His ears get warm. The melody is singing, until it spirals down at last to a pianissimo—barely audible, lovely as a distant bell.

Number of Words: 1444 ÷ _____ Minutes Reading Time = Rate _____

I. VOCABULARY

Circle the meaning of the italicized word as it is used in the following sentences in the selection:

1. Watts makes one *slip* on this old, brassy piano.
   a. fall   **b.** mistake   **c.** tell without meaning to
2. The *passage* is from Schubert's *B-flat Impromptu.*
   a. hallway   **b.** part of a musical work   **c.** voyage
3. "You can *stake* your life on it."
   a. bet   **b.** wooden post   **c.** support
4. Watts lives in New York City and, at least five weeks a year, in a 6-acre *spread* in upstate New York.
   a. open out   **b.** expanse of land   **c.** bed covering
5. "I really believe that all people are born with that ability—to live life creatively, to the *hilt.*"
   a. sword handle   **b.** fullest   **c.** dagger

8 points for each correct answer   SCORE:_____

II. MAIN IDEA

In each group of sentences below, one sentence states a main idea and the other two illustrate or support it. Circle the letter (a, b or c) that states the main idea.

1. **a.** What Houdini had was guts—that is the name of the game.
   b. "Magic is all explainable, you see!" he exclaims.
   c. He is fascinated by Harry Houdini and takes great pleasure in talking about the secrets of the magician's acts.
2. **a.** "I sit at the piano and I'm really all there."
   b. "The ideal musical performer is two people."
   c. "But at the same time there's another me at my shoulder, saying, 'You're going too fast.'"

10 points for each correct answer   SCORE:_____

III. REFERENCE

Which of the reference books listed (a, b, c or d) would you consult first to find the following information required by each statement?

a. atlas   **b.** encyclopedia   **c.** dictionary   **d.** almanac

_____ **1.**   The meaning of the word *pianissimo*.

_____ **2.**   Awards given to musicians in 1979.

_____ **3.**   Cities Watts might include on a tour of Europe.

_____ **4.**   General information about Leonard Bernstein.

5 points for each correct answer   SCORE:_____

IV. SKIMMING

Skim the selection to see how quickly you can find the answer to each of the following questions.

1.   How long has Watts been playing on the stage? _____

2.   Where was Watts born? _____

3.   Who first called on Watts to play with the New York Philharmonic?_____

4.   Who does Watts consider to be his "only real teacher"?

_____

5 points for each correct answer   SCORE:_____

PERFECT TOTAL SCORE: 100   TOTAL SCORE:_____

V. QUESTIONS FOR THOUGHT

What lessons did you learn from reading about Watts? If you did not learn anything, what criticism would you have of his life?

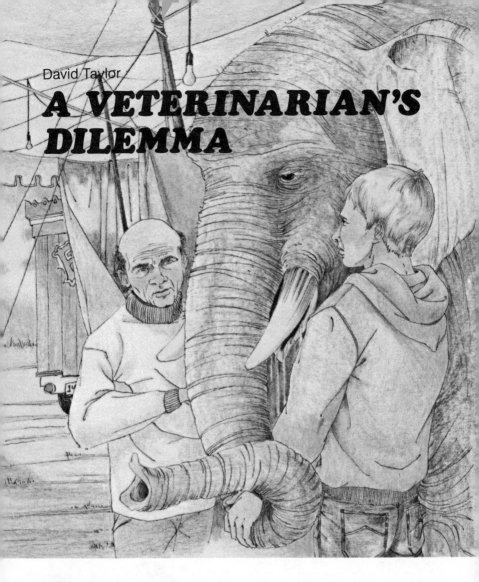

David Taylor

A VETERINARIAN'S DILEMMA

Even as a schoolboy I took an interest in everything that flew, swam or crawled. There was no end of creatures in trouble. Homework would be forgotten as I tried to aid a sick sheep with things from the family medicine cabinet, or patched the hole in a turtle shell with the inner-tube rubber in my bicycle repair kit. But as the years went by, I found myself drawn more and more toward the care of wild, sometimes rare, animals.

Today, my veterinary practice specializes in such animals, mostly in circuses and zoos. This particular time, the call was from a circus in Great Yarmouth, a holiday town on the wind-washed east coast of England. The sick animal was an elephant thought to have foot-and-mouth disease. I had never seen a live case and had only heard of a few cases in elephants.

I drove over and soon found the elephant at the circus. An old German, who turned out to be the elephant trainer, greeted me.

"I am Herr Hopfer," he said. "Please, *Doktor*, come zis way. Gerda iss very ill."

Gerda the elephant was standing in a pool of water that streamed slowly from her lower lip down to the floor. The water was her own saliva. I had to look inside her mouth, but didn't want to stick my hand

blindly into an elephant's mouth.

"Get her to open up, Herr Hopfer," I said.

"Gerda, *auf, auf!*" the trainer shouted.

She raised her trunk, and I shone a flashlight in her pink mouth. No blister in sight.

We checked her feet, looking at her neatly filed and oiled toenails. Nothing that looked like blisters there.

"Now, Herr Hopfer," I said, "tell me the full story."

"Zis morning I find her streaming from ze mouss like zis. She vill not eat, not even drink. Maybe she hass a bad tooss."

Toothache was indeed a possibility. I got Hopfer to make Gerda open her mouth again and shone my flashlight carefully on each tooth with one hand while pressing down the slippery ball of her tongue with the other. I felt Gerda's glands, ran my hands over the outside of her throat, took her tempera-

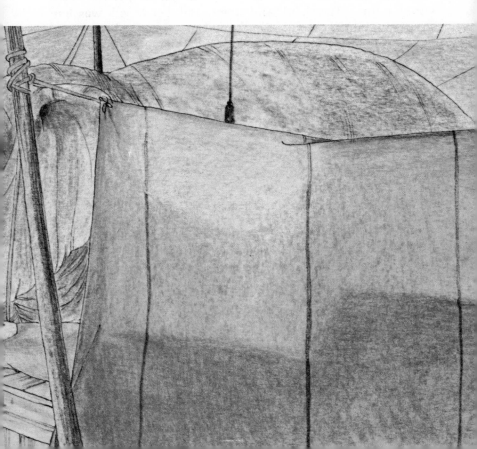

ture and drew a blood sample. Everything was okay. But Gerda's saliva ran and ran.

"Bring me some bananas and a bucket of water," I said to Hopfer. I wanted to watch her reaction to food very carefully for myself.

Gerda took a peeled banana with her trunk tip, popped it in her mouth and swallowed readily. Then slowly, slowly, the pulped banana came back and dripped from the corners of her lips. I put the bucket of water in front of her. She sucked up a trunkful and squirted it into her mouth. She swallowed. In a moment the water gushed back out.

"What did you feed the elephants last thing yesterday, Herr Hopfer?"

"Chopped carrots and apples," he answered.

That was it! I was certain now that one of the apples was jammed somewhere in the gullet. It would be in one of three places: where the gullet enters the chest; where it passes over the heart; or where it pierces the diaphragm. Wherever it was, Gerda was in big trouble.

In cattle, jammed objects often pass naturally if the animal is left alone for 24 hours. That was my first hope. I booked in at a nearby hotel and made

sure that the elephant at least had plenty of water to suck up. Maybe a trickle would get past the apple.

But the next day Gerda was much worse—sunken-eyed, weak and very thirsty. How could I move the apple? If I pushed it somehow, I could tear something. Operating was out of the question; no machine could keep the six-ton monster's lungs full of oxygen when the chest was opened.

By the third day Gerda's eyes were red. her breath was foul and the river of saliva flowed on. She was now desperately thirsty. I tried injecting water and sugar. Nothing seemed to help the beast.

By the fifth day the elephant was going fast. I walked along the shore that morning and thought long and hard. Then I decided. I would dope Gerda lightly, pass a *probang,* a long, hollow leather tube with a brass end, down her gullet and take her life in my hands.

I gave the elephant a big dose of a strong drug. After half an hour she sank to the ground and lay, still drooling, on her side. Herr Hopfer pulled the upper jaw and a helper tugged on the lower. I pushed the probang, greased with cod-liver oil, carefully to the back of Gerda's throat.

A couple of feet of tube disappeared, and suddenly it would go no farther. I marked the tube, withdrew it and measured it against the elephant's body. The mark on the tube told me that the apple was jammed at the point where the esophagus passes the great heart. I must push it on.

I pushed in the probang again, and it stopped once more at the same place. The next strong shove could stop the heart. It could burst the gullet and send the apple into the chest. Or it could succeed.

Gritting my teeth, I increased pressure on the probang. All at once it began to move freely. Something had given. Had the apple moved on or was it now bobbing around on the lungs with a ragged hole in the gullet beside it?

I slowly withdrew the probang until its shining brass end flopped out of Gerda's mouth.

Waiting for the drug to wear off seemed to take forever. But, at nine o'clock that night, Gerda rose sleepily to her feet.

I shouted for a bucket of hay tea (a combination of hot water and new meadow hay) and placed it in front of Gerda. Her trunk flapped weakly. I grabbed it and stuck it into the golden liquid. The bucket half emptied. Gerda's slow and unsteady trunk curled toward her mouth and sprayed in its contents. A wave passed down her throat. She had swallowed. We waited, frozen like statues.

"A banana, a banana!" I shouted frantically.

Herr Hopfer ran for a bunch of fruit. I stuffed a banana straight into the elephant's jaw without peeling it. A moment later it was gone. Still weak, she reached slowly—but eagerly—for more bananas.

That night I stayed up with Gerda, making sure that she was not overloaded too suddenly with food or water. By day she was better, and I went back to my hotel.

"Ooh!" said the waitress as I slumped wearily into my chair at the breakfast table. "Been out on the town, eh? Knew you'd have a smashin' time here in Great Yarmouth. Must be all play, your job!"

Number of Words: 1143 ÷ _____ Minutes Reading Time = Rate _____

I. SEQUENCE

Number the following events from 1 to 6 in the order in which they take place in this selection.

_____ **a.** Toothache was indeed a possibility.

_____ **b.** All at once it began to move freely. Something had given.

_____ **c.** The call was from a circus in Great Yarmouth, a holiday town on the wind-washed east coast of England.

_____ **d.** By the fifth day, the elephant was going fast.

_____ **e.** I marked the tube, withdrew it and measured it against the elephant's body.

_____ **f.** I gave the elephant a big dose of a strong drug.

5 points for each correct answer   SCORE: _____

II. PROBLEM SOLVING

Four of the sentences below trace the veterinarian's thinking in diagnosing and curing the ailing elephant. Put a check √ before each of these sentences.

_____ **1.**   The veterinarian's practice was in England.

_____ **2.**   The elephant could not have foot-and-mouth disease, as had been thought, because no blisters were present.

_____ **3.**   Since Gerda's last meal had been apples, one of them must be jammed somewhere in the gullet.

_____ **4.**   The next day Gerda was sunken-eyed, weak and very thirsty.

_____ **5.**   I was certain now that one of the apples was pinned somewhere in the gullet.

_____ **6.** The apple had to be pushed on, even at the risk of killing the elephant; it was her only hope.

_____ **7.** The waitress thought that the vet had been out on the town.

15 points for each correct answer   SCORE: _____

III. SUMMARY

Read the three statements below. Put a check √ before the one that gives the best summary of the selection.

_____ **1.** Saving the life of Gerda was a great challenge to the veterinarian, but his skill and concern enabled him to see the case through to a happy ending.

_____ **2.** A boyhood interest in animals led the author to become a veterinarian, specializing in circus and zoo animals.

_____ **3.** Many people think that a veterinarian's job is all play and no work.

10 points for correct answer   SCORE: _____

PERFECT TOTAL SCORE: 100   TOTAL SCORE: _____

IV. QUESTIONS FOR THOUGHT

In risking the elephant's life the way he did, how was the veterinarian yet acting professionally? How should he have felt if the elephant had died? Why?

"Where are the mummies?" cry people visiting museums. In fact, mummies are apt to steal the show in these great halls of culture. Not only wide-eyed children, but grown-ups from every walk of life crowd silently around them, wondering what to make of fellow humans dead these last few thousand years. "People are mad about our mummies," says the curator of one small-town museum.

Mummies are messengers from a lost world. Though silent, they tell us much about the long-ago civilization from which they came.

Mummies are important reminders. Through the years they have been studied and "read" by experts, aided by X-rays, photographic lenses, microscopes, tape measures, computers—and an interest in learning more about the past.

The attempt to keep human remains from decomposition is shared by many people. Christ's body was embalmed with "a mixture of aloes and myrrh" according to the Gospel of St. John. When Spanish soldiers entered the royal palace of Peru, they came upon the bodies of dead Inca rulers, seated on thrones! Alexander the Great was preserved in

MUMMIES:

MESSENGERS FROM THE PAST

Ernest Hauser

honey; Lord Nelson, in brandy. In modern times, both Russia's Lenin and China's Mao Tsetung have been preserved.

But it was ancient Egypt that made this art so perfect. Pitting will and knowledge against time, the people of Egypt took on Eternity itself—and nearly got away with it. While many mummies crumble into dust at the first touch, others have lasted through the centuries, as if time had stood still.

A mummy is a corpse saved from decay through a drying process. It was the desert, pressing in on the green strip in which they lived, that gave Egyptians the idea of preserving bodies. The sands, warmed by dry air, were Egypt's earliest cemetery. There, 5000-year-old "nature-made" mummies have been lifted from shallow desert graves where they were buried without coffins. In time, the Egyptians buried their dead in sealed tombs, beyond the reach of prowling beasts. The next step was to match the desert's kindly trick of preservation. Thus the skill of making mummies developed by a trial-and-error process in which people copied nature. The oldest complete mummies known to exist date from the Fifth Dynasty—about 2500 B.C.

Though make-believe mummies have been used in horror movies, the real thing is not so scary. Wrinkled, darkened, their bodies set in timeless sleep, most mummies show a human side. They smile, frown, gape, look pleased, or simply dream. Male mummies usually have their arms crossed over their chests; females have their arms along their sides. There are mummies of priests and priestesses, of landowners, royal treasurers and harem songstresses. There is a mummy of a woman who died in childbirth—her child's little bones laid next to her. A highborn lady, rather than being wrapped, wears her best dress of finely pleated linen. And, in the famous upper room of Cairo's Egyptian Museum, glass-covered oak coffins hold 20 pharaohs and seven

Mummy Case

An artist's conception of the ancient Egyptian process of embalming

queens—a real royal all-star gathering!

The purpose of a mummy is to preserve a person's identity beyond death. When, in 1976, the mummy of Ramses II arrived in Paris for restoration, the French did the right thing by giving him a royal welcome. Flown in from Cairo in a French army jet, His Majesty— the first royal mummy ever to leave Egypt—faced a lineup of the Republican Guard. Ramses' problem, called "museum illness," was caused by colonies of airborne fungi that found their way into his showcase. Eighty-nine harmful kinds were eating into him. French experts treated him successfully with cobalt-60 radiation and sent him home.

The art of making mummies is surprisingly well documented. We know that it was a large, busy industry, using countless craftsmen whose skills were passed on from father to son. The classic eyewitness account, written by Herodotus, the Greek "Father of History," in the 5th century B.C., explains that there were three types of funeral procedures. For the expensive first-class funeral, bearers carried the body to a ferry on the Nile. Transported to the western shore, the body was carried in an elaborate procession, headed by a priest, to a special tent.

The first step was to clean the body. While priests chanted, craftsmen went to work. The chief embalmer wore a jackal's mask—perhaps, at first, a reminder of days when jackals nosed around the desert graves, but later a likeness of the jackal-headed god Anubis, who led dead souls to the afterlife.

Next came the ripper. With a stone blade, he made a cut on the left side of the stomach, leaving a wound 5 inches (12.5 centimeters) long. He would then run as fast as he could, followed by flying rocks and shouts—a token punishment for having violated a human body. Other workers then pulled out the organs, and placed them in four stone jars to be buried with the mummy. The brain was carefully removed. Only the heart was left in place; the seat of the conscience, it would be weighed in the Beyond. The empty body was rinsed with palm wine and coated with liquid resins as a protection against parasites.

The human body is about three-quarters water. How to remove that water without damaging the tissues was the mummy-makers' secret. Modern scientists believe that dry natron, a natural substance containing sodium bicarbonate and sodium chloride, was tightly packed around the body. It would take up to 40 days to draw out liquids. This length of time is mentioned in Genesis. Joseph, on Jacob's death in Egypt, "commanded his servants, the physicians, to embalm his father . . . and 40 days were fulfilled for him; for so are fulfilled the days of those which are embalmed."

Next the body was filled with linen packages, or sawdust, to give it back its roundness. The wound on the side was covered with a gold plate; toes and fingernails were painted with henna; ladies' hair was braided; and valuable

Artistic likenesses of Egyptian royalty guard entrance of ancient Abu Simbel Temple

stones were placed in the eye sockets. Often the cheeks were padded from within to give the deceased a more lifelike appearance. Indeed, great care was taken to keep the facial features, chief proof of who the dead person was. The body was then rubbed with aromatics—still sniffable in many specimens—and coated with a layer of hard resin.

The clean shell of what was once a person could now safely be wrapped up. The wrapping might take two weeks. Up to 150 yards (137 meters) of linen bandages were used. Sometimes there was a colorful arrangement of contrasting bands on the outside.

Once the 70-day process was finished, the "Opening of the Mouth" ceremony took place. It was thought that this rite allowed the dead to breathe, eat, drink and go before the Judge. The mummy was held upright while a priest touched its bandaged face saying, "You're alive! You're young!" And so, at last, after a grand feast given by family and friends, the mummy could be laid to rest. Kings and queens, as a rule, were buried by themselves. The well-off had their family tombs. The ragged mummies of the poor were stacked in crowded mass graves.

The ancient Egyptians believed that the mummy would

now begin a dark journey through the underworld. Its destination: the Judgment Hall of Osiris, son of Sky and Earth. The human mummy was supposed to resemble Osiris, no doubt to gain his favor. But getting to Osiris was far from easy. The journey took the dead through terrifying pits of darkness. Demons attacked the mummy's boat. It had to pass through a gate guarded by two fierce serpents. If all went well, it finally came face to face with stern Osiris, who, with the help of 42 assistants, ordered the weighing of its heart.

Inside its bandages, the dead person carried a scarab, a sacred beetle carved in costly stone. On it was a message to the heart asking it "not to bear witness" against the owner. Still, if the dead person's heart was weighed down by evil deeds, no scarab could save the sinner. He or she would be quickly eaten by the crocodile-headed Eater of the Dead. The others would march on to lasting joy in a delightful never-

An Egyptian mummy appearing today as it did at time of burial over two thousand years ago

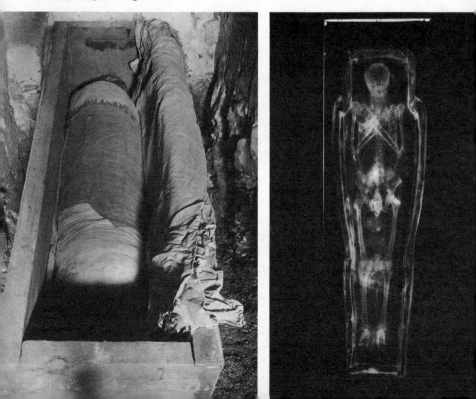

never land that looked much like Egypt.

To make the dead feel at home in their afterlife, tombs were carved and painted with scenes of the good life. They were filled with food and drink, furniture, toilet articles (including combs and razors) and, for the rich and mighty, golden treasure—the idea perhaps being, "You *can* take it with you!"

In search of such treasure, grave robbers tunneled their way into tombs whenever they could find them. Even the royal dead buried in tombs driven deep into limestone cliffs were not safe. Sealed by pieces of rock and built with shafts, false doors and tricky turns, the mummies rested in secret rooms, often hundreds of feet inside the mountain. Still they were ransacked, probably by the very workmen who had built them.

When Napoleon Bonaparte, then a young general, invaded Egypt in 1798, he brought with him a team of scientists, who

Studies of mummies by modern scientists disclose secrets of ancient Egypt.

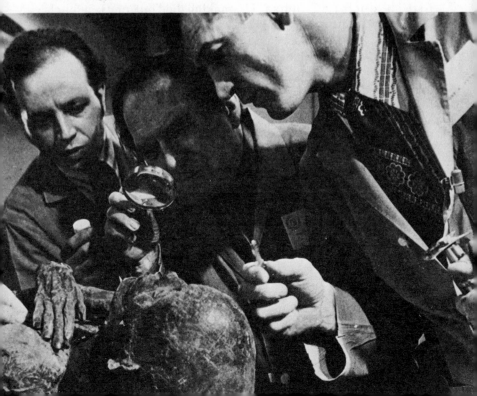

made the first real study of Egyptian treasures. The mummies they unearthed amazed them. Ears, noses, cheeks, lips, eyelids—all had a "natural appearance." Each hair was "solidly implanted!"

The French expedition caused a culture shock. Europe went Egypt-crazy overnight. Napoleon himself is said to have brought back two mummies for the drawing room of Josephine, his wife and the future empress of France.

As mummies by the hundreds began to arrive at museums, a passion for these dead Egyptians swept over people. A British doctor, Thomas J. ("Mummy") Pettigrew, bought mummies at $150 apiece and stripped them of their bandages in front of paying audiences. Meanwhile, a big business in fake mummies sprang up around Egyptian tourist sites.

Today, Egypt forbids the export of mummies, hundreds of which are still coming to light. As they do, mummies are filling gaps in our knowledge of the past. Thanks to them, we know that a person's life under the pharaohs lasted about 35 years; that Egypt's ladies dyed their black hair blonde; that toothaches bothered Egyptians from the pharaoh on down. A research party from the University of Michigan's School of Dentistry, working in Cairo, has come up with a list of tooth problems that would keep any modern dentist busy! Almost every ill we suffer existed in ancient Egypt.

Violence was part of this life too. One pharaoh was found to have a big ax wound in his forehead. A prince's twisted face points to his death by poison.

Before the art of mummy-making died out, one last touch was added—the mummy portrait. Painted on a thin wooden panel, it was attached to the mummy's banded face. Many of these surprisingly "modern" likenesses are so realistic that even the stubble on a young man's chin is not forgotten. They suggest that the deceased is peering out from his cocoon as through a window. Eyes bright, lips slightly parted, the mummy seems to say, "Look, here I am—surviving death!"

Number of Words: 1874 ÷ _____ Minutes Reading Time = Rate _____

I. FACT/OPINION

Write F before each sentence that states a fact. Write O before each sentence that states an opinion.

_____ **1.**   Mummies are the best part of a museum exhibit.

_____ **2.**   Ancient Egypt perfected the art of making mummies.

_____ **3.**   A mummy is a corpse saved from decay through a drying process.

_____ **4.**   The oldest complete mummies known to exist date from 2500 B.C.

_____ **5.**   Mummies are not unpleasant to look at.

_____ **6.**   The French did the right thing by giving the mummy of Ramses II a royal welcome.

_____ **7.**   The human body is about three-quarters water.

_____ **8.**   A mummy seems to say, "Look, here I am, surviving death!"

5 points for each correct answer   SCORE:_____

II. SUPPORTING DETAILS

In each group of sentences below, one sentence makes a general statement and the other two support it. Circle the letter of the general statement.

1. **a.** Tombs were decorated with scenes of the good life.
   b. Food and drink were buried with the mummies.
   c. Egyptians wanted to make the dead feel at home in their afterlife.
2. **a.** Mummies are filling holes in our knowledge of the past.
   b. Egypt's ladies dyed their black hair blonde.
   c. The length of life under the pharoahs was 35 years.

10 points for each correct answer   SCORE:_____

III. OUTLINING

Complete the outline below by writing the correct answer of 1, 2, 3 or 4 in its proper place.

1. The art of making mummies is well documented.
2. A portrait painted on wood was often attached to the mummy's banded face.
3. They tell us much about a long-ago civilization.
4. Skills were passed on from father to son.

I.   Mummies are messengers from a lost world.

    A.   _____

    B.   Many mummies have lasted through the centuries.

II. The purpose of a mummy is to preserve a person's identity beyond death.

    A.   _____

    B.   The mummy of Ramses II was given a royal welcome by the French in 1976.

    C.   Cairo's Egyptian Museum contains the mummies of 20 pharoahs and seven queens.

III. _____

    A.   It was a large industry using countless craftsmen.

    B.   _____

    C.   Herodotus wrote an eyewitness account of it.

---

10 points for each correct answer   SCORE:_____

PERFECT TOTAL SCORE: 100   TOTAL SCORE:_____

IV. QUESTION FOR THOUGHT

Why do you suppose the practice of mummification was abandoned by civilizations that once practiced it?

Diana Nyad

BEYOND ALL LIMITS

Record breaking long distance swimmer, Diana Nyad, counting strokes

Eight thousand four hundred. Should I ask the time? No. I know the time. Five hours, 36 minutes. Six hundred strokes to go, 24 minutes. Hang on. Stay strong. Finish strong. Four hundred one, two, three. . . ."

I was finishing my last training swim in June 1974. Fifteen

miles (24 kilometers) in Lake Ontario. My trainer, Cliff Lumsdon, was next to me in the motorized inflatable "Rubber Ducky." He steered the course, kept me away from floating debris and tourist boats, and clocked my miles as we reached the markers. But I didn't need to be told how fast I was going or how far I had gone. I set a rhythmic, balanced pace of 2.5 miles (3.6 kilometers) per hour and never wavered. Six hundred strokes to the mile, every mile in 24 minutes. Fifteen miles (24 kilometers) in six hours. Nine thousand strokes.

I glided one stroke past the last marker, floated on my back for 30 seconds, then pulled my goggles up onto my forehead with a sigh and a smile. Cliff pulled me into the "Rubber Ducky," wrapped me in towels and we putted back home, grinning all the way. The exhausting work was over. Miles and miles of slow distance, September through December. Races in South America, January and February. Sprints and more work in the pool, March and April. Outdoor training with Cliff, May and June. Hours every day. Thoroughly tired every day. Bored with the repetition. Fed up with the inflexible eat-sleep-swim routine. This 15-mile (24-kilometer) workout marked the welcome end of many trying months. On the next day I was leaving for Italy. There was to be a race across the Bay of Naples, and I was ready.

My plane was scheduled for 4:30 p.m. I slept in until 7 a.m. and looked forward to an unusual day of relaxation. Cliff went to work and said he would pick me up at 2:45. I packed, ate, read and at noon decided to go for a loose preflight swim in Lake Ontario. The sun was hot; kids were playing up and down the bluff. I asked a couple of boys if they would watch my towel and sneakers for an hour. One said, "You're not going in the lake, are you?" I smiled and went to the water's edge. The water washed up over my feet; I caught my breath and jumped back. "Come on, Nyad. This hour will do you good, help you relax, calm you down. Get in there!"

I dived in and my heart stopped. Depending on wind direction, Lake Ontario can undergo extreme temperature changes of up to 20° Fahrenheit (-5° Celsius) within 24 hours. And this water, I knew, was not the 61° Fahrenheit (16° Celsius) of yesterday. Far from it. I would go 1000 strokes straight out and 1000 back. One hour, eight minutes.

A thousand strokes usually takes me just over a mile and a half (2.4 kilometers). I stopped at the count and realized I had barely moved. My arms had been spinning to keep warm. My legs were immobile and folded up under my chest. By the time I maneuvered around to face the shore, I discovered I had traveled a mere 400 yards (366 meters). I was scared. My jaw opened and locked, my throat was rigid and unable to scream and my fingers were spread and useless. I began an inefficient breaststroke and, in half an hour, made half the distance. Two hundred more yards (183 meters), but I couldn't move. Barely keeping myself afloat, bobbing lower and lower, I was hit by the very strong possibility that I was about to drown.

Another attempt at a scream, but all my breath seemed to be caught in my mouth, and no sound would come. Some signal must have traveled, how-

Diana enjoys the welcome feeling of relief after vigorous workout.

ever, because I saw the kids running up and down the shore, waving their arms and yelling for help.

Hope renews strength; I was moving forward again. I had made it to 40 yards (37 meters) from shore, when a man came bounding over the bluff, splashed into the water and was out to me within 30 seconds. From behind, he threw his arms over my shoulders, hooked his hands in my armpits and lifted me onto a sunbaked rock. I was shivering nonstop, moaning instead of talking; and by the time the ambulance came I realized that the warmth of this man's hands had burned the front of my shoulders. His hands, at 98.6° Fahrenheit (38° Celsius), had left two bloody wounds. What could the water temperature have been?

I warmed up in a body oven, and a doctor bandaged my shoulder wounds and called the Coast Guard for me. The lake was 40° Fahrenheit (5° Celsius). Forty degrees! I had nearly drowned, I had missed the plane to Rome, but all I could think of was beating Lake Ontario.

I felt like a boxer who had taken a beating yet couldn't wait to climb back into the ring. I wanted Lake Ontario. Five people had crossed it south to north. No mean feat. Thirty-two miles (52 kilometers) across a cold, wavy and very fickle Great Lake. But they had been helped in part by the strong currents of the Niagara River that shoot north into the lake for about 5 miles (8 kilometers). Always looking for the near-impossible dream, I asked Cliff if anyone had ever swum the lake north to south. He shook his head. It would be tricky fighting those northbound Niagara River currents after you had made it most of the way across—just when you were weakest. I said that I wanted to make a double crossing: first the hard way, north to south, then back the "easy" way. Cliff laughed; but when our eyes met, he reached out and shook my hand. We would go after Lake Ontario together.

I was late reaching Italy; the burns were slow to heal. But the race went in my favor anyway. I broke the world's record and crossed the Bay of Naples in 8 hours 11 minutes. I recovered, got my weight and strength back, and entered five more races, one each weekend. The fifth was on a Sunday, 25 grueling miles (40 kilometers) across a cold lake in northern

Quebec. By the following Thursday, I was supposed to be in Chicago for a Lake Michigan race. After that, there would be an ocean swim down the west coast of Mexico.

I never showed up in Chicago, nor in Mexico. It was a difficult decision because the races meant money, as well as points for world standing. But it was the second week of August, and I knew that by September it would be impossible to swim Lake Ontario.

So Cliff and I began planning the incredible 64-mile (103 kilometer) two-way crossing. You couldn't see the floor for the charts. Counters and tables were cluttered with coffee cups, grease jars and glucose bottles; bathing suits hung from every doorknob. The phone rang all day. Every television and radio station, every newspaper and magazine in Toronto, wanted a story on the crazy girl from New York.

An old friend of Cliff's agreed to help us with the charts for currents and to navigate on the day of the swim. With his radar-equipped boat, he would be 100 yards (91 meters) ahead of us, changing the course according to crosswinds or headwinds. The navigator's vessel is especially helpful at night; we simply follow the green light at the top of his mast. An escort boat would be about 30 yards (27 meters) off my right, carrying equipment and serving as resting place for the crew. The "Rubber Ducky" would be on my left, so that when I lifted my face to breathe, I could swim in a straight line by checking my distance from the boat. If anyone needed to relay information to me, a whistle would be blown, and I would pause in mid-breath just long enough to read a huge blackboard. To feed, I would swim close to the "Rubber Ducky" and pick up cups of hot glucose.

Cliff, as chief trainer, would be next to me all the time. Cliff's daughter would be the pacer, coming in to swim with me for half an hour at a time every five or six hours when I reached the desperate low points. Two of the Lake Ontario frogmen would be running the "Rubber Ducky," prepared for emergencies or repairs. And my four best buddies would be there to help Cliff and to lend much-appreciated support. The rest was up to me.

Mid-August is usually the point in the swimming season when I am at my absolute strongest. I had trained like a bandit for nine months, competed in six very tough races and rested for a full week. If anybody could make this swim, I could. The weather was right on the 16th. We set the starting time for seven o'clock the next morning.

Up at 4:30. Six raw eggs, cereal, toast with honey, hot liquid protein with glucose. Fill the thermoses, double-check the supplies, run through the signals. I am thoughtful on the morning of a swim. I know too well what lies in store for me. By 6:00, the crew is loading the boats. I pose, joke, talk to the press. At 6:50, greasing begins. Everyone shouts best-of-luck phrases. I make a final adjustment of the goggles and take the plunge.

It is a beautiful, clear day. Water temperature, 72° Fahrenheit (22° Celsius) Outside the harbor, the lake is almost as smooth as glass. For the first three hours, I make incredible progress. Stroking strongly, 60

Diana walking ashore after swim across Lake Ontario and before attempting swim back to Toronto

strokes to the minute, doing my counting tricks to pass the time, stopping for 10 seconds every hour on the hour to down the glucose drink.

A headwind comes up during the fourth hour. A 2-foot (1.2-meter) chop. This wind increases steadily during the next six hours. By the 10th hour, I am fighting 6- and 7-foot (1.8 to 2.1 meters) waves. My arms are weakened from slapping and punching walls of water. I am shivering with the cold. The water temperature has dropped to 63° Fahrenheit (19° Celsius). The grease has for the most part washed off, and I realize I'm not even close to the other shore. I will not, however, let doubt take its turn in my mind. A pacer would be helpful at this point, but I decide to wait for the return trip. I can't afford to worry about getting over when I still face the long trip back.

Fear comes quickly on the heels of self-doubt. Fear that I

am not worthy of the goal, that my commitment has been too heavy, that I may end up looking like a quitter by chasing such an unreasonable dream. This is the first sign that intense concentration and mental control will be needed for every coming minute.

Fear, doubt and boredom are major battles for the long-distance swimmer. Even during a short period of time—such as an hour—the mind begins to wander. And 12, 20 or 30 hours of continual stress can become the greatest test.

Dark goggles over the eyes. The head turns some 60 times a minute toward a boat for direction, but the eye is almost never focused. Tight rubber caps block out most hearing. Both tactile sense and balance are seriously distorted. In short, for 30 hours you are left with nothing at all but your own thoughts. You must keep your will strong enough to resist the pains that bombard you; but you must fill your mind with something other than pain itself. After a few hours into a difficult swim, your mind begins to drift; the danger comes when it drifts so far that you lose touch with what you're doing—which makes it impossible to continue, to watch the boat every stroke, to come in for the feedings, to remember why you are going through this agony.

I use a singing-counting technique to stay alert. The goal of my 15th hour was 75 rounds of "Frère Jacques."

Shortly after my 15th feeding I catch a glimpse of lights from the shore. It is 10 p.m. I ask Cliff and he reaffirms. We are getting there. Still, we must take the bad with the good. The currents from the Niagara River are reaching to push me away, and they become stronger and stronger as we approach the shore. I am shaking uncontrollably, and soon currents push me one stroke back for every two I take forward. I don't complain; I don't speak at all. Head down, arms weak but steady—very determined.

At 1:20 a.m. I touch the shore after 18 hours and 20 minutes of nonstop swimming. I am frozen, my legs can't support me, my arms feel bruised from battling the waves for so many hours. Even though I am preparing for the return trip, which must begin in 10 minutes, I allow myself a moment of glory in knowing that I am the first and only person to have crossed this brutal lake north to south. Reporters zero in, and people press close to catch a glimpse of me.

They rope off a small square on the beach, like a boxing ring. They sit me in a chair, regrease me, feed me some solid food, change my caps and post me on the time every 30 seconds.

Cliff knows better than anyone that I am utterly exhausted. I have lost a great deal of weight and strength. He whispers softly in my ear, "You just completed a great swim; you don't have to get back in there if you don't want to."

But I have to try. I walk back into the water at 1:30 a.m. I am chilled to the bone, but I start stroking and after an hour or so I feel better. During a breath I yell that I'm going to make it. Cliff gives me the thumbs-up sign. All my friends cheer. Horns blare from the flotilla of boats that have come with us through the night. At 20 hours, 30 minutes—24 miles (39 kilometers) from victory—I lose consciousness.

In my heart, the Lake Ontario swim was a success. A grand success. Against nearly impossible odds, I made it to the south shore and had the courage to walk back into that frozen dark for the return trip. That's what those people waiting on the shore admire—the courage. The utter exhaustion, and the courage it stands for, is an inspiration to everyone who witnesses it.

I think of the emotional response of these people on the shore as one kind of payment. The big reward, of course, is in my heart, my head. When I finish these grueling swims, I feel I have performed superhuman feats. I create boundless confidence for the future. And part of the satisfaction comes from public approval. Marathon swimming is not a multimillion-dollar sport; the people who wait for me, who applaud me when I'm still a mile out, are a reward in themselves. I remember their eyes, their faces, their voices—and the memory is as clear as that of my own rush of success. Sometimes I walk out of the water on my own; often I need help, and once in a while, I leave the scene on a stretcher. They are always there. They yell, "Bravo, Diana!" "Fantastic!"

Number of Words: 2608 ÷ _____ Minutes Reading Time = Rate _____

I. LANGUAGE USAGE

Circle the letter of the word or phrase (a, b or c) that correctly states the meaning of the italicized word in each sentence.

1. I set a pace and never *wavered*.
   a. trembled   **b.** varied from it   **c.** lost my balance
2. Crossing Lake Ontario was no *mean* feat.
   a. difficult   **b.** unusual   **c.** ordinary
3. I had trained *like a bandit* for nine months.
   a. like a crook   **b.** informally   **c.** very hard
4. I stopped to *down* the glucose drink.
   a. swallow   **b.** prepare   **c.** warm
5. When I finish these *grueling* swims, I feel I have performed superhuman feats.
   a. competitive   **b.** very long   **c.** exhausting

8 points for each correct answer   SCORE:_____

II. GENERALIZATIONS

Certain generalizations may be made based on the information in this selection. Put a check √ before each of the three sentences that makes such a generalization.

_____ **1.** Long-distance swimmers must train constantly to keep in shape.

_____ **2.** A training swim should be at least 15 miles.

_____ **3.** Six hundred strokes to the mile is the average for a long-distance swimmer.

_____ **4.** Marathon swimmers often become multimillionaires.

_____ **5.** Much of the satisfaction a swimmer gets comes from public approval.

10 points for each correct answer   SCORE:_____

III. SUPPORTING DETAILS

In each set of three sentences below, one sentence makes a general statement and the other two support it. Circle the letter of the general statement.

1. **a.** After swimmers are in the water many hours, their senses can become seriously distorted.
    b. Tight rubber caps block out most hearing.
    c. Dark goggles cover the eyes.

2. **a.** The radar on board helps keep us on course.
    b. The navigator's vessel is especially helpful.
    c. The green light at the top of the mast is followed by the swimmer at night.

3. **a.** Diana and Cliff began planning the crossing.
    b. Counters and tables were cluttered with coffee cups.
    c. You couldn't see the floor for the charts.

10 points for each correct answer   SCORE:_____

PERFECT TOTAL SCORE: 100   TOTAL SCORE_____

IV. QUESTIONS FOR THOUGHT

Is it sensible for people like Diana Nyad to deliberately inflict on themselves the punishment of long-distance swimming? Why do you think they do it?

WORLD'S FIRST AND GREATEST DETECTIVE

James Stewart-Gordon

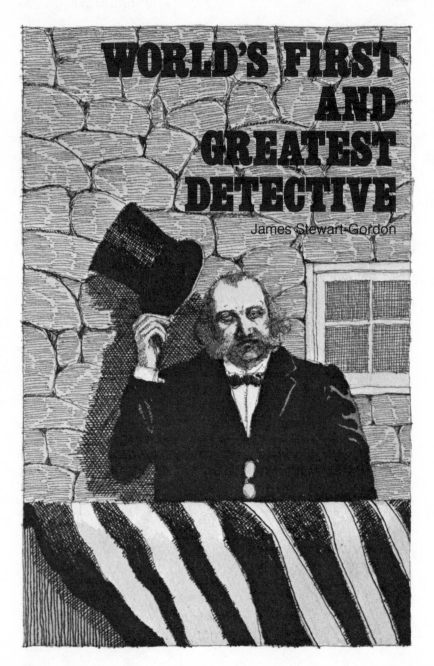

"I am Vidocq!" the incredible Frenchman would announce. François-Eugène Vidocq lived a life so filled with adventure, romance and accomplishment that he can only be described as a combination of Sigmund Freud, Casanova, Houdini and J. Edgar Hoover. He was, in turn: a soldier, victim of a frame-up, a man on the run trying to clear his name, an unwilling companion of robbers and murderers, an honest businessman, a police spy and the world's first real detective. The *Sûreté,* which he started in 1812 and headed until 1827, is the model for the Criminal Investigation Department of England's Scotland Yard, our own FBI and every other department of criminal investigation in the world.

Vidocq was also the man writer Edgar Allan Poe had in mind when he wrote about Chevalier Dupin in "Murders in the Rue Morgue." There is also much of Vidocq in Sir Arthur Conan Doyle's character Sherlock Holmes and in Agatha Christie's now famous detective Hercule Poirot.

It is believed that Vidocq was responsible for the arrest of at least 20,000 criminals. Indeed, so fearless and clever was this one-man answer to crime that crooks trembled at the drop of his name. Once, he was sent to storm Paris's well-known robbers' den. Some of the most dangerous criminals in Europe lived there. When an official said that Vidocq would need 1000 policemen, Vidocq smiled. "Monsieur," he said, "I shall need only eight."

On the night of the raid, Vidocq left his men outside with a bag of handcuffs and walked into the robbers' den alone. Big and important-looking, dressed in black, he climbed the bandstand. "Stop the music," he shouted. The music stopped.

"I am Vidocq!" were his next words. Knives and guns, already drawn, fell to the floor. At his direction, the robbers quietly formed a line. Then, as they moved to the door, he used a piece of chalk to put a cross on the back of those he wanted arrested or held for questioning. Outside, the marked men were handcuffed and taken off to jail.

"Amazing," said the official when he heard about the raid. Vidocq shrugged. "A day's work," he said.

Long before there were crime labs, Vidocq made sure that every object found at the scene of a crime was studied under a microscope. From his own studies and knowledge of crime, Vidocq stated: "Criminals are not inventive. If they pull a job and it is successful, they will soon use the same method again." So he and his men kept files of criminals by name, type of crime, habits, methods and pals. In time these files included almost every known criminal in France. Vidocq thus began a system that today serves as a model for the criminal-records departments of every major police force in the world.

HUNTED MAN

François-Eugène Vidocq was born in Arras, France, July 23, 1775. He was the son of a baker. By the time he was 14, he was a master swordsman. His father decided that the boy needed discipline and sent him to the army. The year was 1789. In Paris the Bastille had fallen. The bloodbath of the French Revolution was at hand.

According to his own story, Vidocq's soldier years were full of glory. But after years of fighting, he tired of the army, returned to Arras, married and set up as a shopkeeper. Howev-

er, he was soon arrested and imprisoned for leaving the army. In prison, two men accused him of a crime they themselves had committed. They lied, and Vidocq was unable to defend himself against their charges and clear his name. Rather than face more prison, Vidocq made his escape—and became a hunted man.

UNDERCOVER AGENT

The next ten years were a nightmare of captures, imprisonments and escapes. It was during the years Vidocq spent in prison and on the run that he began to build his big store of knowledge about criminals and crime. And all the while he kept looking for the men who had done him in. Finally, in 1799, when he was arrested in Lyons, he met Dubois, the head of the Lyons police. Vidocq told him his story. "I must have my freedom," he begged, "so I can prove I am innocent!"

Dubois offered a free pass out of Lyons if Vidocq would use his knowledge of the underworld to help run down a gang of robbers. In no time the robbers were caught and Vidocq had his freedom.

Hoping to make a fresh start, Vidocq changed his name, got false papers and set up a clothing shop in Versailles. But one day Vidocq came face to face with a pair of former fellow prisoners who said they would tell people about his past. This time, Vidocq told his story to Monsieur Henry of the Paris police. If Henry would help him, he would enter prison and act as a spy. Henry agreed to the undercover arrangement.

For 21 months Vidocq re-mained behind bars, sending information to Henry, who could then make many arrests. Once out of prison, Vidocq be-came a police agent, with the power of arrest.

During his years in hiding, Vidocq had become good at disguise. Now he used this tal-ent in his job for the police. As

the daring Jules, a strong-arm man, he entered the hideouts of killers. As Jean-Louis, a seller of stolen goods, he got to know robbers. And as a tottering old gentleman looking for a young wife, he got to know the women who hung around with criminals. His success in these roles was outstanding.

LAST SECRET

In the time of peace that followed the fall of Napoleon, Paris drew criminals from every corner of the world. Vidocq felt that the police methods then in use were not good enough. So he started a special

Vidocq in three of his various disguises

criminal department of his own. The force, which was to work under cover and include mostly ex-criminals, was called the Sûreté.

Among the ex-cons hired by Vidocq were Fouché, a powerful man as fearless as Vidocq himself; Goury, once a swindler; Ronquetti, a cardsharp; Aubé, an ex-forger; and the sneakthief Coco Lacour. By 1820, eight years after its start, this tough lineup had grown into a 30-man team. Vidocq's men cut the Paris crime rate by 40 percent. And Vidocq received a full pardon for his earlier problem with the law.

NEW CAREER

At the age of 52, Vidocq began the first book on crime and criminals written by a professional detective. It was an immediate best-seller. In 1834 he founded the Information Bureau, the first private-eye and credit-reporting service in the world. It soon had 3000 clients.

Vidocq still helped the police on their hard cases. He solved his last crime at 80. A company had some unexplained losses.

Vidocq talked to the staff, asked a few questions and then pointed to the bookkeeper, an extremely ugly woman. It turned out that she had been giving the money to her young, handsome boyfriend. "How did you know?" everyone asked. Vidocq gave a shrug: "Messieurs," he said, "only a woman who has a boyfriend wears expensive perfume at nine in the morning. If this lady had a boyfriend, it could only be someone she was giving money to."

To the very end, Vidocq remained an exciting figure in Paris, a storyteller who delighted writers like Balzac and Dumas with his stories. And always he kept up his habit of dining with the beautiful young women of Paris. To each he told his last secret—that she was the one true love of his life and would inherit his money.

At 82, he slipped away peacefully one bright morning, leaving behind him a legend, the start of the science of criminology, and 11 beautiful women. When his will was read, they learned that he had left his fortune to his housekeeper.

Number of Words: 1315 ÷ _____ Minutes Reading Time = Rate _____

I. SUPPORTING DETAILS

Read the general statement below about the life of François-Eugène Vidocq. Three of the sentences that follow the general statement give details that support it. Check √ each of these three.

> Vidocq lived a life so filled with adventure, romance and accomplishment that he can only be described as a combination of such greats as Sigmund Freud, Casanova, Houdini and J. Edgar Hoover.

_____ **1.** Vidocq kept up his habit of dancing with the beautiful young ladies of Paris.

_____ **2.** Vidocq climbed the bandstand and shouted, "Stop the music!"

_____ **3.** It is believed that Vidocq was responsible for the arrest of at least 20,000 criminals.

_____ **4.** Vidocq was sent to the army when he was 14 years old.

_____ **5.** Vidocq became a master of disguises.

5 points for each correct answer   SCORE:_____

II. CHARACTERIZATION

Put a check √ before seven adjectives below that might be applied to Vidocq. Be prepared to defend your answers.

___ **a.** withdrawn   ___ **e.** dishonest   ___ **i.** cruel
___ **b.** adventurous   ___ **f.** knowledgeable___ **j.** timid
___ **c.** fearless   ___ **g.** romantic   ___ **k.** self-confident
___ **d.** undisciplined___ **h.** successful   ___ **l.** exciting

5 points for each correct answer   SCORE:_____

III. CRITICAL THINKING

Check √ three statements that most clearly show the author expressing a strong personal opinion.

_____ **1.** Vidocq was a victim of a frame-up.

_____ **2.** Vidocq was a spy and the world's first detective.

_____ **3.** He became a police agent with the power of arrest.

_____ **4.** Crooks trembled at the drop of his name.

_____ **5.** His success in these roles was terrific.

10 points for each correct answer   SCORE:_____

IV. MAIN IDEA

Circle the letter (a, b or c) of the sentence that gives the main idea in each group below.

1. **a.** As Jean-Louis, Vidocq got to know robbers.
    b. During his years in hiding, Vidocq had become good at disguises.
    c. He entered the hideout of killers as daring Jules, a strong-arm man.
2. **a.** He solved his last crime at the age of 80.
    b. He kept up his habit of dining with the beautiful young ladies of Paris.
    c. To the very end, Vidocq remained an exciting figure.

10 points for each correct answer   SCORE:_____

PERFECT TOTAL SCORE: 100   TOTAL SCORE:_____

V. QUESTIONS FOR THOUGHT

If Vidocq's life were to be made into a television series, what incidents would you dramatize? Why?

FRONTIERS OF THE MIND

Laile Bartlett

correctly named the number.

These events are examples from the world of Psi (psychic phenomena)—something that cannot be explained by known science or the laws of nature.

Today, some scientists tell us that Psi is our new frontier. They see a future world where we can be in touch with others around the globe and move through time and space with a leap of the mind. They say we will know the future and the past as well as the present, and cure our own ills through the power of the mind. Whatever the future brings, we are now in the middle of a great Psi explosion.

In 1969 the American Association for the Advancement of Science accepted parapsychologists (people who study psy-

While eating lunch at school one day, a 13-year-old boy "heard" his little sister at home screaming. Knowing that his mother was out of the house, he ran home and found that the child had been badly cut. The boy called a doctor, who came in time to save the child from bleeding to death.

In a carefully prepared experiment, a Miss Z was put to sleep in a lab. Electrodes recorded her brain waves. Miss Z was asked to "read" a five-digit number put on a shelf high over her head. While kept in her bed by the medical equipment, she "floated up" and

chic phenomena) as members. Their Psi SEARCH exhibit is being shown at museums, universities and libraries across the country. It is supported by the Smithsonian Institution.

SEARCH shows 40 years of photographs and reports about psychic phenomena. Researchers are trying to find out what is valuable and proven about Psi and what is just a good guess.

Psi is indeed a subject that people talk and argue about. Fakes can take advantage of confused and eager seekers. For many people, Psi opens a closet they would rather keep shut: "My dreams keep coming true. Am I going crazy?"

Psi has not been very welcome in the scientific world. Paul Kurtz, a professor of philosophy, speaks for many doubting scientists when he says: "We are bothered that only so-called positive results are published. The public hardly ever hears about negative findings, and there are many." Another expert, Stanley Krippner, disagrees: "In the ten years of our work in Psi and dreams at Maimonides Medical Center in Brooklyn, we published all our results, negative or positive. For many years

Psychic phenomena is now being subjected to scientific research under laboratory conditions.

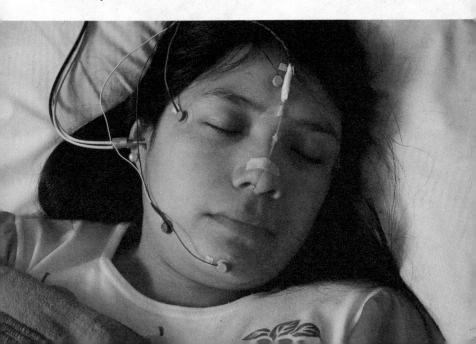

Researchers use elaborate instruments in their investigations of psychic phenomena.

parapsychologists have been the outcasts of science." He then goes on to add, "Fortunately, this is changing because of recent improvements in experimentation."

Pinning down psychic phenomena is a slow, exacting process. Because the whole field is on trial, serious Psi researchers are very careful with their methods and slow to make reports of their findings. Still, from their experiments, here is what we do know:

TELEPATHY

People can and do communicate with one another by means other than the five senses. When one mind is com-

DIVISION OF
PARAPSYCHOLOGY
&
PSYCHOPHYSICS

municating with another mind, they are using telepathy.

Telepathy comes through in everyday events and serious warnings. For instance, a waitress "gets a message" and hands a man his order before he gives it. A Texas teacher breaks a rule and leaves her students to be near the telephone. It rings: "Come at once," says the caller. "Your sister is dying."

Sometimes, in the lab telepathy works *too* well. Krippner tells about a lab subject who sensed his experimenter's need for $25 to pay a bill!

CLAIRVOYANCE

People can and do pick up information on faraway or hidden things, persons or events. This is called clairvoyance.

Under laboratory controls at Stanford Research Institute, scientists studied the clairvoyant Uri Geller. A picture was hidden in two sealed envelopes. Geller drew the exact picture. He did this experiment correctly seven times in a row. An object was hidden in one of ten sealed cans. Geller picked the correct can. He did this experiment ten times without a mistake. The odds: one in a billion!

The same lab also found clairvoyant abilities in six people who had not had any experience before. All of them were able to describe in detail distant "target areas" picked by the scientists.

PRECOGNITION

People can and do sense what is going to happen before

it takes place. This is called **precognition.**

In one of the 15,000 cases gathered by researcher Louisa Rhine, a 19-year-old California girl changed her plans to go to a funeral. A premonition told her that she "had" to get to her mother. When she got home, her parents were sitting in the living room. She "had" to get them out of their chairs. She said she was hungry and talked them into joining her in the kitchen. No sooner had they left the living room, than a car crashed into the house. It destroyed the chairs in which her parents had been sitting.

So close have some "hunches" been that precognition listings have been set up in New York and California. These listings contain predictions made by people about major events. A few of the "hits" in these precognition files: space-program failures and Martin Luther King's assassination.

PSYCHOKINESIS

People can and do move or affect objects, even distant ones, without touching them. This phenomenon is known as psychokinesis.

Felicia Parise watched a film of a Russian woman, Nina Ku-lagina. In the film Nina moved objects by gestures or with her eyes. Felicia, a staff member of the Maimonides Dream Laboratory in Brooklyn, New York, then performed some of the same things under controlled conditions.

Bernard Grad at McGill University in Montreal, Canada, got some seeds "treated" by a healer. He wet them and put them in a dish to grow. At the same time he wet some other seeds not "treated" by the healer. The "treated" seedlings grew faster, and their plants weighed more at the end of the carefully watched experiment.

What is known about how these four Psi phenomena work? Under what conditions are they most successful? Some discoveries so far:

1. Distance doesn't seem to matter. Psi has been recorded in the same room and from outer space.

2. People who believe in Psi, or want it to work, usually do better at it.

3. People who feel close to each other appear to communicate better.

4. Shock events, such as accidents and disasters, come through—or at least are reported—much more often than normal or happy ones.

5. Psi works better in states such as deep relaxation, hypnosis and sleep. Most of the reported cases of precognition are in dreams.

A major puzzle is *how* to get scientific proof for Psi. The very tools that would document psychic phenomena are based on the old understanding that scientific fact is only what you can measure and observe. However, such material by its very nature resists capture, often going dead or turning off in a lab situation. Many people are instantly held back when hitched up to a machine in a booth.

Olga Worrall, a psychic healer from Baltimore, recalls: "The first time I concentrated on a damaged leaf for a healing experiment (at U.C.L.A.), I 'burned it up.' I had to 'tone down' for the lab. Most of those who can work at all in a lab tend to taper off after a time—what scientists call the "decline effect."

Psychic Ingo Swann is a good example of this. Though he has been very successful as a subject in lab experiments— for instance, changing temperatures on instruments by force of will—it seems that such feats reveal only a portion of his psychic ability.

In out-of-body experiments Swann can "go" to any spot on the globe, given its latitude and longitude, and sketch correctly the mountains, rivers, roads and buildings just as they are at that point.

When asked in an experiment in New York to "go" to a hidden box and describe its contents, Swann said, "You forgot to turn on the light in the box. It's dark." He was correct!

But these are small accomplishments compared to what Swann and others seem able to do on their own. Once, bored by months of lab work in California, Swann phoned his friend Harold Sherman, 1500 miles (2414 kilometers) away in Arkansas, and suggested they take a 600-million-mile (965-million-kilometer) trip together. They would "go" to Jupiter, which neither of them knew anything about. They did know that *Pioneer 10* was scheduled to pass Jupiter in the near future. Sherman agreed.

The next day, both Swann and Sherman filed reports of their trip. The colors: landscapes, atmosphere and other conditions they described were surprisingly similar. Nor were they far off from the information *Pioneer 10* later brought back about Jupiter.

The planet Jupiter as seen by space craft Pioneer X

Challenged by a science editor, Swann and Sherman then turned their attention to Mercury. *Mariner 10* was soon to pass this planet. At the time, most scientists believed that Mercury had neither atmosphere nor magnetic field. Yet both Swann and Sherman reported a thin atmosphere and a magnetic field. So did *Mariner 10* later that month.

We may not know exactly *what* Psi is, or exactly *how* it works, but we do know *that* it works. And as practical people we are already employing it.

In detective work. A major chain of stores in Toronto, Canada, hired a man with precognitive abilities to spot people

about to shoplift. He's correctly spotted thousands—even predicting *what* they will take minutes before they take it.

Psychic Gerard Croiset of Utrecht, the Netherlands, is noted for solving many crimes. He can pick up cues on the telephone. Once, called upon to help find a missing man, Croiset was able to say that the man was dead. His description of the place was so accurate that police found the body later that day.

In locating resources. Clairvoyance is now being used to find water, minerals and treasures. On play-by-play instructions from psychic Aron Abrahamsen, a scientist dug up deeply buried objects in Flagstaff, Arizona. The objects were over 100,000 years old. Of Abrahamsen's 58 predictions that were tested 51 have proved correct. "Psi is replacing the spade as archeology's primary tool," says one scientist.

In health work. Psychic healing may become common someday. It is thought that 70 percent of illnesses are brought on by stress and by thinking oneself sick. "If you can think yourself sick, why not think yourself well?" asks one doctor. He is part of a growing group that uses "holistic" medicine (how all aspects of medicine fit together) based on the power of consciousness to influence the body. "Treating disease through the mind is the coming thing in medicine," he declares.

"One can become aware of the flow of energy within oneself and use it," says Jack Schwarz. He can control his body much as do the yogis in India. He can stick a knitting needle through his arm, with no pain or bleeding. The wound closes when the needle is withdrawn and heals completely within a day or two. A number of researchers believe that this self-healing ability can be learned.

Beyond all this, Psi presents us with hints of a universal unity. It was this Oneness that struck astronaut Edgar Mitchell on his trip to the moon, "merging the boundaries of the self with the cosmos." Then and there, Mitchell pledged his life and career to the understanding of consciousness and what that could mean to the human condition. "We can't all go to the moon," he admits, "but perhaps the deeper awareness of Psi processes can provide the same perspective."

People were surprised when Copernicus, the astronomer, said that the earth circles the sun. But the new view won out.

We may be at another such turning point today. In the words of Willis Harman of Stanford Research Institute: "Psychic research in the next few decades may be destined to have an impact comparable to the impact a few centuries ago of Galileo and Copernicus. I call it the Second Copernican Revolution."

Number of Words: 2004 ÷ _____ Minutes Reading Time = Rate _____

I. AUTHOR'S PURPOSE

Put a check √ in front of the sentence that the author used to demonstrate the amazing results of psychic powers.

_____ 1. People who believe in Psi, or want it to work, usually do better at it.

_____ 2. While kept in her bed by the medical equipment, she "floated up" and correctly named the number.

_____ 3. Today some scientists tell us that Psi is our new frontier.

_____ 4. Psi works better in states such as deep relaxation, hypnosis and sleep.

15 points for correct answer   SCORE: _____

II. FACT/OPINION

Write whether each sentence below is a fact (F) or an opinion (O).

_____ 1. It's impossible for people to communicate by other means than the five senses.

_____ 2. A number of researchers believe that self-healing ability can be learned.

_____ 3. Psi is our most important frontier.

_____ 4. Parapsychologists are now accepted by other scientific organizations.

_____ 5. Treating disease through the mind is the coming thing in medicine.

_____ 6. Many experiments are now being done in the field of psychic phenomena.

10 points for each correct answer   SCORE: _____

III. VOCABULARY

Match each Psi term in column A with the correct definitions in column B by copying letter in space provided.

	A		B
_____ **1.**	psychokinesis	**a.**	one mind communicating with another mind
_____ **2.**	clairvoyance	**b.**	sensing what is going to happen before it takes place.
_____ **3.**	precognition	**c.**	gaining information on remote or hidden objects, persons, or events.
_____ **4.**	telepathy	**d.**	moving or affecting objects without touching them.
_____ **5.**	psychic phenomena	**e.**	something that cannot be explained by known science or the laws of nature.

5 points for each correct answer   SCORE: _____

PERFECT TOTAL SCORE: 100   TOTAL SCORE: _____

IV. QUESTION FOR THOUGHT

Do you agree or disagree with the belief that psychic phenomena may one day be accepted as valid by everyone? Give reasons for your answer.

Eric J. Alava

OLD UGLY WAS A GOOD FRIEND

We were scuba diving at Whale Cove, a small inlet on the coast of Oregon, when I first came across Old Ugly, a wolf eel lying at the entrance of his cave. The sun filtered down through the water and glistened off his grayish-white face.

As I slowly swam toward him, his black eyes followed me, while his jaws moved in a chewing motion. Finally, when I was within a few feet of the fish, he backed off into the black recess of his rock home. This was the first of many meetings with Old Ugly, as he came to be called.

The wolf eel, whose scientific name is *Anarhichthys ocellatus,* is commonly found in the bays along the coast of Washington and Oregon. It makes its home in underwater rock crevasses, old tires, or under any solid object it can squeeze into. The normal diet of the wolf eel is shellfish, and dungeness crabs are a special delicacy. Its powerful jaws handle the biggest crabs with ease. The larger eels grow to a length of 8 feet (2.5 meters), and may weigh over 20 pounds (9 kilograms). The ferociousness of this fish when attacked, speared, or hooked on a line has been witnessed by many divers and fishermen. However, it rarely attacks other creatures unless it is looking for a meal.

Whenever we dove in Whale Cove, we would check to see how Old Ugly was getting along. Eventually we discovered that he shared his rock pile with an octopus, who lived directly under him. The two had formed a harmonious relationship. On one visit, I saw the eel bring home a good-sized crab, which he ate on his front porch. As pieces of crabmeat and shells drifted to the bottom near the front door of the octopus, a slender tentacle would slither out of the hole and delicately pick up any edible tidbits.

One day a fellow diver, Ed Sieffert, offered Old Ugly a piece of fish on the end of his knife. After some coaxing and with the temptation of meat so near his mouth, he took it. Ed noticed the octopus below watching sorrowfully, so he dropped him a piece of fish, too. After that it became a common practice for divers to feed Old Ugly and the octopus. Soon it got to the point that when we made a dive near his rock pile, the eel would happily come snaking through the water, looking for a handout.

These good times went on throughout the summer. Old Ugly and his silent partner, the octopus, became living legends with the local divers. After a dive in Whale Cove, the divers would retire to a favorite restaurant and, over drinks, would tell tales about the two neighbors in Whale Cove. It was funny how the size of both the eel and the octopus grew with the telling of the stories.

Once I went down to the cove with Bill Herder, a longtime diver and owner of a local dive ship. He wanted to photograph Old Ugly. We swam down to the cave, and there

was our favorite wolf eel, but with some company—a young female, who stayed in the background. Bill got into position, inserted a flashbulb and took a photograph. When the bulb went off, Old Ugly thought he was being attacked, so he and his girlfriend made a counterattack. For a while all that could be seen were fins, bubbles and the dark bodies of the eels churning in the water. We made a hasty retreat, with only our dignities harmed. Bill later showed me some close-up slides of wolf eels attacking the flashbulbs.

Later that summer, Old Ugly was as friendly as ever. The

female had left him, the mating season being over. The octopus still lived in the downstairs apartment and, by this time, was so used to seeing us that he hardly changed colors when we neared his territory.

Then, one fall day, when the sky was overcast with early storm signs of winter and the breaking waves were rolling in a little larger than usual, we went down to Whale Cove. The wind blew in from the sea, pelting us with stinging salt water. As we approached the jumping-off point where the sea meets the cliff walls, I saw a diver struggling in the water. He made it to the shore, with a large spear gun in his arms. He was pulling on the line that was attached to a long spear. The spear was embedded in a crea-ture thrashing about on the jagged rocks in death agonies. It was Old Ugly.

We ran toward him, but the diver had sunk his knife into the wolf eel's brain before we could reach him. The jaw stopped its chewing motion; the piercing eye slowly glazed over; the body relaxed and was still. The diver, a stranger, noticed us. He held up the massive old head, now covered with blood and sand. "Biggest eel I ever saw," he said. "It swam right up to me. What an easy shot!"

The rains started, and the dark swells whipped the water's surface into foam. The breakers rolled in and crashed onto the rocks. We didn't make a dive that day, but not because of the weather or the sea.

Number of Words: 888 ÷ _____ Minutes Reading Time = Rate _____

I. SEQUENCE

Number these events from the selection in the order in which they happened.

_____ **a.** Then one fall day they saw another diver carrying a large spear gun.

_____ **b.** His knife sank into the wolf eel's brain.

_____ **c.** The divers discovered a wolf eel, which they nicknamed Old Ugly.

_____ **d.** It became a common practice for the divers to feed Old Ugly and the octopus, too.

5 points for each correct answer   SCORE: _____

II. INFERENCES

Read each question below. Then draw a circle around the letter (a, b or c) of the sentence that provides the best answer to the question.

1. What kind of relationship did the divers have with the wolf eel and the octopus?
   a. They feared the creatures but would not admit it.
   b. They enjoyed watching the two creatures.
   c. It made them feel brave to know the creatures feared them.

2. Why was Old Ugly such an easy target for the diver who killed him?
   a. The diver probably offered it some food as bait.
   b. Its eyesight was poor, and the water was very murky.
   c. It was used to being fed by divers, and was not afraid.

3. How do you think the others felt about what had happened?
   a. They felt responsible, because they had taught the eel not to fear humans.

b. They were relieved that the creature had not suffered.

c. They wondered what would become of the octopus now.

10 points for each correct answer   SCORE: _____

III. CLASSIFYING

Put each statement below into one of the following categories:

a. Where wolf eels live.

b. What wolf eels eat.

c. How wolf eels look.

d. How wolf eels act.

e. How wolf eels eat.

_____ **1.** It rarely attacks other creatures unless it is looking for a meal.

_____ **2.** The larger eels grow to a length of 8 feet (2.5 meters) and may weigh over 20 pounds (9 kilograms).

_____ **3.** Its powerful jaws make it possible to handle the biggest crabs with ease.

_____ **4.** The wolf eel is commonly found in the bays along the coast of Washington and Oregon.

_____ **5.** The normal diet of the wolf eel is shellfish, and dungeness crabs are a special delicacy.

10 points for each correct answer   SCORE: _____

PERFECT TOTAL SCORE: 100   TOTAL SCORE: _____

IV. QUESTIONS FOR THOUGHT

What do you think is the most interesting part of this story? Why?

A SEPARATE PEACE

Tom Stoppard

CAST: John Brown
                Nurse
                Doctor
                Nurse Maggie Coates
                Matron
                Nurse Jones

SCENE 1: *The office of the Beechwood Nursing Home. Behind the reception counter sits a uniformed nurse. It is 2:30 a.m. A car pulls up outside. John Brown enters. He is a biggish man, with a well-lined face: calm, pleasant. He is wearing a nondescript suit and overcoat, and carrying two zipped traveling bags. Looking around, he notes the neatness, the quiet, the flowers, the nice nurse, and is quietly pleased.*

BROWN: Very nice.

NURSE: Good evening. . . .

BROWN: Evening. A lovely night. Morning.

NURSE: Yes . . . Mr. . . . ?

BROWN: I'm sorry to be so late.

NURSE: *(shuffling papers)* Were you expected earlier?

BROWN: No. I telephoned.

NURSE: Yes?

BROWN: Yes. You have a room for Mr. Brown.

NURSE: Oh!—Have you brought him?

BROWN: I brought myself. Got a taxi by the station. I telephoned from there.

NURSE: You said it was an emergency.

BROWN: That's right. Do you know what time it is?

NURSE: It's half past two.

BROWN: That's right. An emergency.

NURSE: *(aggrieved)* I woke the house doctor.

BROWN: A kind thought. But it's all right. Do you want me to sign in?

NURSE: What is the nature of your emergency, Mr. Brown?

BROWN: I need a place to stay.

NURSE: Are you ill?
BROWN: No.
NURSE: But this is a private hospital . . .
         (BROWN *smiles for the first time*)
BROWN: The best kind. What is a hospital without priva-
         cy? It's the privacy I'm after—that and the clean lin-
         en . . . (*A thought strikes him*) I've got money.
NURSE: . . . the Beechwood Nursing Home.
BROWN: I require nursing. I need to be nursed for a bit. Yes.
         Where do I sign?
NURSE: I'm sorry, but admissions have to be arranged in
         advance except in the case of a genuine emergency—
         I have no authority—
BROWN: What do you want with authority? A nice person
         like you. (*Moves*) Where have you put me?
NURSE: (*moves with him*) And *you* have no authority—
BROWN: (*halts*) That's true. That's one thing I've never had.
         (*He looks at her flatly*) I've come a long way.
NURSE: (*wary*) Would you wait for just one moment?
BROWN: (*relaxes*) Certainly. Have you got a sign-in book?
         Must abide by the regulations. Should I pay in
         advance?
NURSE: No, that's quite all right.
BROWN: I've got it—I've got it all in here—
(*He starts trying to open one of the zipped cases, it jams and he
hurts his finger. He recoils sharply and puts his finger in his
mouth. The* DOCTOR *arrives, disheveled from being roused*)
NURSE: Doctor—this is Mr. Brown.
DOCTOR: Good evening. What seems to be the trouble?
BROWN: Caught my finger.
DOCTOR: May I see?
(BROWN *holds out his finger: the* DOCTOR *studies it, looks up:
guardedly*)
DOCTOR: Have you come far?
BROWN: Yes. I've been traveling all day.
(*The* DOCTOR *glances at the* NURSE)
BROWN: Not with my finger. I did that just now. Zip stuck.
DOCTOR: Oh. And what—er—
NURSE: Mr. Brown says there's nothing wrong with him.

BROWN:	That's right—I—
NURSE:	He just wants a bed.
BROWN:	A room.
DOCTOR:	But this isn't a hotel.
BROWN:	Exactly.
DOCTOR:	Exactly what?
BROWN:	I don't follow you.
DOCTOR:	Perhaps I'm confused. You see, I was asleep.
BROWN:	It's all right. I understand. Well, if someone would show me to my room, I shan't disturb you any further.
DOCTOR:	*(with a glance at the* NURSE*)* I don't believe we have any rooms free at the moment.
BROWN:	Oh yes, this young lady arranged it.
NURSE:	He telephoned from the station. He said it was an emergency.
DOCTOR:	But you've come to the wrong place.

BROWN: No, this is the place all right. What's the matter?

DOCTOR: *(pause)* Nothing—nothing's the matter. *(He nods at the nurse)* All right.

NURSE: Yes, doctor. *(Murmurs worriedly)* I'll have to make an entry . . .

DOCTOR: Observation.

BROWN: *(cheerfully)* I'm not much to look at.

NURSE: Let me take those for you, Mr. Brown. *(The cases)*

BROWN: No, no, don't you. *(Picks up cases)* There's nothing the matter with me. . . .

(BROWN *follows the* NURSE *inside. The* DOCTOR *watches them go, picks up* BROWN's *form, and reads it. Then he picks up the phone and starts to dial)*

SCENE 2: BROWN's *private ward. A pleasant room with a hospital bed and the usual furniture. One wall is almost all window and is curtained.* BROWN *and the* NURSE *enter.* BROWN *puts his cases on the bed. He likes the room.*

BROWN: That's nice. I'll like it here. *(peering through curtains)* What's the view?

NURSE: Well, it's the drive and the gardens.

BROWN: Gardens. A front room. What could be nicer?

*(*NURSE *starts to open case)*

NURSE: Are your night things in here?

BROWN: Yes, I'll be very happy here.

*(*NURSE *opens the case, which is full of money—bank notes)*

NURSE: Oh—I'm sorry—

*(*BROWN *is not put out at all)*

BROWN: What time is breakfast?

NURSE: Eight o'clock.

BROWN: Lunch?

NURSE: Twelve o'clock.

BROWN: Tea?

NURSE: Three o'clock.

BROWN: Supper?

NURSE: Half past six.

BROWN: Cocoa?

NURSE: Nine.

BROWN: Like clockwork. Lovely.

(The DOCTOR *enters with* BROWN's *form and adhesive bandage)*

DOCTOR: Excuse me.

BROWN: I was just saying—everything's A-1.

DOCTOR: I remembered your finger.

BROWN: I'd forgotten myself. It's nothing.

DOCTOR: Well, we'll just put this on overnight.

(He puts on the adhesive strip)

DOCTOR: I expect matron will be along to discuss your case with you tomorrow.

BROWN: My finger?

DOCTOR: . . . Well, I expect she'd like to meet you.

BROWN: Be pleased to meet her.

SCENE 3: *The hospital office. It is morning, and the* DOCTOR *is at the desk, telephoning.*

DOCTOR: . . . I have absolutely no idea. . . . The nurse said it looked like rather a lot. . . . His savings, yes. No I don't really want the police turning up at the bedside of any patient who doesn't arrive with a life history. . . . I think we'd get more out of him than you would, given a little time. . . . No, he's not being difficult at all. . . . You don't need to worry about that—he seems quite happy. . . .

SCENE 4: BROWN's *private ward.* BROWN *is in striped pajamas, eating off a tray. A second nurse—*NURSE COATES (MAGGIE)*—is waiting for him to finish so that she can take his tray away.* MAGGIE *is pretty and warm.*

BROWN: The point is not breakfast in bed, but breakfast in bed without guilt—if you're not ill. Lunch in bed is more difficult, even for the rich. It's not any more expensive, but the disapproval is harder to ignore. To stay in bed for tea is almost impossible in decent society, and not to get up at all would probably bring in the authorities. But in a hospital it's not only understood—it's expected. That's the beauty of it. I'm not saying it's a great discovery—it's obvious really: but I'd say I'd got something.

MAGGIE: If you'd got something, there wouldn't be all this fuss.

BROWN: Is there a fuss? (MAGGIE *doesn't answer*) I'm paying my way. . . . Are you pretty full all the time?

MAGGIE: Not at the moment, not very.

BROWN: You'd think a place as nice as this would be very popular.

MAGGIE: Popular?

BROWN: I thought I might have to wait for a place, you know.

MAGGIE: Where do you live?

BROWN: I've never lived. Only stayed.

MAGGIE: You should settle down somewhere.

BROWN: Yes, I've been promising myself this.

MAGGIE: Have you got a family?

BROWN: I expect so.

MAGGIE: Where are they?

BROWN: I lost touch.

MAGGIE: You should find them.

BROWN: (smiles) Their name's Brown.

(The MATRON enters: she is not too old, and quite pleasant)

MATRON: Good morning.

BROWN: Good morning to you. You must be matron.

MATRON: That's right.

BROWN: I must congratulate you on your hospital, it's a lovely place you run here. Everyone is so nice.

MATRON: Well, thank you, Mr. Brown. I'm glad you feel at home.

(MAGGIE *takes* BROWN's *tray*)

BROWN: I never felt it there. Very good breakfast. Just what the doctor ordered. I hope he got a bit of a lie-in.

(MAGGIE *exits with the tray, closing the door*)

MATRON: Now, what's your problem, Mr. Brown?

BROWN: I have no problems.

MATRON: Your complaint.

BROWN: I have no complaints either. Full marks.

MATRON: Most people who come here have something the *matter* with them.

BROWN: That must give you a lot of extra work.

MATRON: But it's what we're here for. You see, you can't really stay unless there's something wrong with you.

BROWN: I can pay.

MATRON: That's not the point.

BROWN: What is the point?

MATRON: This is a hospital. What are you after?

BROWN: *(sadly)* My approach is too straightforward. An ordinary malingerer or a genuine hypochondriac wouldn't have all this trouble. They'd be accepted on their own terms. All I get is a lot of personal questions. *(Hopefully)* Maybe I could *catch* something. . . . But what difference would it make to you?

MATRON: We have to keep the beds free for people who need them.

BROWN: I need this room.

MATRON: I believe you, Mr. Brown—but wouldn't another room like this one do?—somewhere else? You see, we deal with physical matters—of the body—

BROWN: There's nothing wrong with my *mind*. You won't find my name on any list.

MATRON: I know.

BROWN: *(teasing)* How do you know? *(She doesn't answer)* Go for the obvious, it's worth considering. I know what I like: a nice atmosphere—good food—clean rooms—no demands—cheerful staff— Well, it's *worth* the price. I won't be any trouble.

MATRON: Have you thought of going to a nice country hotel?

BROWN: Different kettle of fish altogether. I want to do nothing, and have nothing expected of me. That isn't possible out there. It worries them. They want to know what you're at—staying in your room all the time—they want to know what you're *doing*. But in a hospital it is understood that you're not doing anything, because everybody's in the same boat—it's the normal thing.

MATRON: But there's nothing wrong with you!

BROWN: That's why I'm *here*. If there was something wrong with me I could get into any old hospital—free. As it is, I'm quite happy to pay for *not* having anything wrong with me.

MATRON: But what do you want to do here?

BROWN: Nothing.

MATRON: You'll find that very boring.

BROWN: One must expect to be bored, in a hospital.

MATRON: Have you been in a hospital quite a lot?

BROWN: No. I've been saving up for it. . . . *(He smiles)*

SCENE 5: *The hospital office. The* DOCTOR *is phoning at a desk.*

DOCTOR: No luck? . . . Oh. Well, I don't know. The only plan we've got is to bore him out of here, but he's disturbingly self-sufficient. . . . Mmmm, we've had a psychiatrist over. . . . Well, he seemed amused. . . . Both of them, actually; they were both amused. . . . No, I shouldn't do that, he won't tell you anything. And there's one of our nurses—she's getting on very well with him . . . something's bound to come out.

SCENE 6: BROWN'S *ward.* BROWN *is in bed with a thermometer in his mouth.* MAGGIE *is taking his pulse. She removes the thermometer, scans it and shakes it.*

MAGGIE: I'm wasting my time here, you know.

BROWN: *(disappointed)* Normal?

MAGGIE: You'll have to do better than that if you're going to stay.

BROWN: You're breaking my heart, Maggie.

MAGGIE: *(almost lovingly)* Brownie, what are you going to do with yourself?

BROWN: Maggie, Maggie . . . Why do you want me to do something?

MAGGIE: They've all got theories about you, you know.

BROWN: Theories?

MAGGIE: Train robber.

BROWN: That's a good one.

MAGGIE: Embezzler.

BROWN: Naturally.

MAGGIE: Eccentric millionaire.

BROWN: Wish I was. I'd have my own hospital, just for my-self—with nurses, doctors, rubber floors, flowers, stretchers parked by the elevators, clean towels and fire regulations.

MAGGIE: It's generally agreed you're on the run.

BROWN: No, I've stopped.

MAGGIE: I think you're just lazy.

BROWN: I knew you were the clever one.

MAGGIE: *(troubled, soft)* Tell me what's the matter, Brownie?

BROWN: I would if there was.

MAGGIE: What do you want to stay here for then?

BROWN: I like you.

MAGGIE: You didn't know I was here.

BROWN: That's true. I came for the quiet and the routine. I came for the white calm, meals on trays and quiet efficiency, time passing and bringing nothing. That seemed enough. I never got it down to a person. But I like you—I like you very much.

MAGGIE: Well, I like you too, Brownie. But there's more in life than that.

(MATRON enters)

MATRON: Good morning.

BROWN: Good morning, matron.

MATRON: And how are we this morning?

BROWN: We're very well. How are you?

MATRON: *(slightly taken aback)* I'm all right, thank you. Well, are you enjoying life?

BROWN: Yes, thank you, matron.

MATRON: What have you been doing?

BROWN: Nothing.

MATRON: Now really, Mr. Brown, this won't do, you know. Wouldn't you like to get up for a while? Have a walk in the garden?

BROWN: No, I suppose not. But I didn't come here for that. I must have walked thousands of miles in my time.

MATRON: It's not healthy to stay in bed all day.

BROWN: What do the other patients do?

MATRON: The other patients are here because they are not well.

BROWN: I thought patients did things . . . *(vaguely)* made things.

MATRON: I suppose you wouldn't like to make paper flowers?

BROWN: What on earth for? You've got lots of real ones.

MATRON: You haven't got any.
BROWN: Well, no one knows I'm here.
MATRON: Then you must tell somebody.
BROWN: I don't want them to know.
MATRON: Who?
BROWN: Everybody.
MATRON: You'll soon get tired of sitting in bed.
BROWN: Then I'll sit by the window. I'm easily pleased.
MATRON: I can't let you just languish away in here. You must do *something*.
BROWN: *(sighs)* All right. What?
MATRON: We've got basket weaving. . . ?
BROWN: Then I'll be left alone, will I?

SCENE 7: *The hospital office. The* DOCTOR *is on the phone.*

DOCTOR: Well, *I* don't know—how many John Browns *are* there in Somerset house? . . . Good grief! . . . Of course, if it's any consolation it may not be his real name . . . I know it doesn't help . . . That's an idea, yes . . . His fingerprints . . . No, no, I'll get them on a glass or something—Well, he might have been in trouble some time. . . .

SCENE 8: BROWN's *ward.* BROWN *is working on a shapeless piece of basketry.* MATRON *enters.*

MATRON: What is it?
BROWN: Basketwork.
MATRON: But what is it for?
BROWN: Therapy.
MATRON: You're making fun of me.
BROWN: It is functional on one level only. If that. *You'd* like me to make a sort of laundry basket and lower my-self in it out of the window. That would be func-

tional on *two* levels. At least. *(Regards the mess sadly)* And I'm not even blind.

(MATRON *silently dispossesses* BROWN *of his basketry)*

MATRON: What about *painting*, Mr. Brown.

(That strikes a chord)

BROWN: Painting . . . I used to do a bit of painting.

MATRON: Splendid. Would you do some for me?

BROWN: Paint in here?

MATRON: Nurse Coates will bring you materials.

BROWN: What colors do you like?

MATRON: I like all colors. Just paint what you fancy. Paint scenes from your own life.

BROWN: Clever! Should I paint my last place of employment?

MATRON: I'm trying to help you.

BROWN: I'm sorry. I know you are. But I don't need help. Everything's fine for me. *(Pause)* Would you like me to paint the countryside?

MATRON: Yes, that would be nice.

SCENE 9: *The hospital office. The* DOCTOR *is on the phone.*

DOCTOR: No . . . well, we haven't got anything against him really. He's not doing any harm. No, he pays regularly. We can't really refuse. . . . He's got lots left. . .

SCENE 10: BROWN's *ward.* BROWN *is painting a landscape all over one wall. He hasn't got very far, but one sees the beginnings of a simple pastoral scene, competent but amateurish.* MAGGIE *enters, carrying cut flowers in a vase.*

MAGGIE: Hello—*(She notices)*

BROWN: I'll need some more paint.

MAGGIE: *(horrified)* Brownie! I gave you drawing paper!

BROWN: I like space. I like the big sweep—the contours of hills all flowing.

MAGGIE: Matron will have a fit.

BROWN: What are the flowers?

MAGGIE: You don't deserve them.

BROWN: Who are they from?

MAGGIE: Me.

BROWN: Maggie!

MAGGIE: I didn't buy them.

BROWN: Pinched them?

MAGGIE: Picked them.

BROWN: A lovely thought. Put them over there. I should bring *you* flowers.

MAGGIE: I'm not ill.

BROWN: Nor am I. Do you like it?

MAGGIE: Very pretty.

BROWN: I'm only doing it to please matron really. I could do with a bigger brush. There's more paint, is there? I'll need a lot of blue. It's going to be summer in here.

MAGGIE: It's summer outside. Isn't that good enough for you?

(BROWN *stares out of the window: gardens, flowers, trees, hills*)

BROWN: I couldn't stay out there. You don't get the benefits.

MAGGIE: *(leaving)* I'll have to tell matron, you know.

BROWN: You don't get the looking after. And the privacy. *(He considers)* I'll have to take the curtains down.

SCENE 11: *The hospital office.*

MATRON: What did the psychiatrist think?
DOCTOR: He likes him.
MATRON: *(sour)* He's likable.
DOCTOR: *(thoughtfully)* I just thought I'd let him stay the
           night. I wanted to go back to bed and it seemed the
           easiest thing to do. I thought that in the morning. . . .
           Well, I'm not sure what I thought would happen in
           the morning.
MATRON: He's not simple—he's giving nothing away. Not even
           to Nurse Coates.
DOCTOR: Well, keep her at it.
MATRON: She doesn't need much keeping.

SCENE 12: BROWN's *ward.* BROWN *has painted a whole wall and is
working on a second one.* MAGGIE *sits on the bed.*

MAGGIE: That was when I started nursing, after that.
BROWN: Funny. I would have thought your childhood was all
           to do with ponies and big stone-floored kitchens. . . .
MAGGIE: Goes to show. What was your childhood like?
BROWN: Young . . . I wish I had more money.
MAGGIE: You've got a lot. You must have had a good job. . . ?
BROWN: Center for the army team.
MAGGIE: You're not fair! You don't give me anything in
           return.
BROWN: This painting's for you, Maggie. . . . If I'd got four
           times as much money, I'd take four rooms and paint
           one for each season. But I've only got money for the
           summer.
MAGGIE: What will you do when it's gone?
BROWN: *(seriously)* I don't know. Perhaps I'll get ill and have
           to go to a hospital. But I'll miss you, Maggie.
MAGGIE: If you had someone to look after you, you wouldn't
           have this trouble.

BROWN: What trouble?

MAGGIE: If you had someone to cook your meals and do your
          laundry, you'd be all right, wouldn't you?

BROWN: It's the things that go with it.

MAGGIE: You should have got married. I bet you had
          chances.

BROWN: Perhaps.

MAGGIE: It's not too late.

BROWN: You don't think so?

MAGGIE: You're attractive.

BROWN: What are you like when you're not in uniform? I
          can't think of you not being a nurse. It belongs to
          another world I'm not part of any more.

MAGGIE: What have you got about hospitals?

BROWN: A hospital is a very dependable place. Anything
          could be going on outside. Since I've been in here—
          there could be a war on, and for once it's got noth-
          ing to do with me. I don't even know about it. Fire,
          flood and misery of all kinds, across the world or
          over the hill, it can all go on, but this is a private
          ward; I'm paying for it. (Pause) The meals come in
          on trays, on the dot—the dust never settles before it's
          wiped—clean laundry at the appointed time—the ma-
          tron does her round, not affected by anything out-
          side. You need never know anything, it doesn't
          touch you.

MAGGIE: That's not true, Brownie.

BROWN: I know it's not.

MAGGIE: Then you shouldn't try and make it true.

BROWN: I know I shouldn't.

(Pause)

MAGGIE: Is that all there is to it, then?

BROWN: You've still got theories?

MAGGIE: There's a new one. You're a retired forger.

BROWN: Ha! The money's real enough.

MAGGIE: I know.

BROWN: How do you know?

MAGGIE: (shamefaced) They had it checked.

(BROWN laughs)

BROWN: They've got to make it difficult. I've got to be a
         crook or a lunatic.

MAGGIE: Then why don't you tell them where you came
         from?

BROWN: They want to pass me on. But they don't know who
         to, or where. I'm happy here.

MAGGIE: Haven't you been happy anywhere else?

BROWN: Yes. I had a good four years of it once.

MAGGIE: In a hospital?

BROWN: No, that was abroad.

MAGGIE: Where have you been?

BROWN: All over. I've been among French, Germans, Greeks,
         Turks, Arabs. . . .

MAGGIE: What were you doing?

BROWN: Different things in different places. (Smiles) I was
         painting in France.

MAGGIE: An artist?

BROWN: Oh very. Green and brown. I could turn a row of
         tanks into a leafy hedgerow. Not literally. Worse
         luck.

SCENE 13: *The hospital office. The* DOCTOR *is on the phone.*

DOCTOR: . . . He meant camouflage. . . . Well, I realize that,
         but there are a number of points to narrow the
         field. . . . Must be records of some kind. . . . Service
         in France and Germany, probably Middle East. . . .

SCENE 14: BROWN's *ward.* BROWN *has painted two walls and is
working on a third.*

MAGGIE: It's very nice, Brownie. Perhaps you'll be famous
         and people will come here to see your mural.

BROWN: I wouldn't let them in.

MAGGIE: After you're dead. In a hundred years.

BROWN: Yes, they could come in then.

MAGGIE: What will you do when you've finished the room?

BROWN: Go back to bed. It'll be nice in here. Hospital routine
in a pastoral setting. That's kind of perfection,
really.

MAGGIE: You could have put your bed in the garden.

BROWN: What's the date?

MAGGIE: The 27th.

BROWN: I've lasted well, haven't I?

MAGGIE: How old are you?

BROWN: Twice your age.

MAGGIE: Forty-four?

BROWN: And more. (*Looking close*) What are you
thinking?

MAGGIE: Before I was born, you were in the war.

BROWN: (*moves*) Yes. Private Brown.

MAGGIE: Was it awful being in the war?

BROWN: I didn't like the first bit. But in the end it was very
nice.

MAGGIE: What happened to you?

BROWN: I got taken prisoner. . . . Four years.

MAGGIE: Is that where you were happy?

BROWN: Yes. . . . Funny thing, that camp. Up to then it was
all terrible. Chaos—all the pins must have fallen off
the map, dive bombers and bullets. Oh dear, yes.
The camp was like breathing out for the first time in
months. I couldn't believe it. It was like winning,
being captured. The war was still going on, but I
wasn't going to it any more. They gave us food, life
was regulated in a way I'd never known, in a box of
earth and wire and sky. On my second day I knew
what it reminded me of.

MAGGIE: What?

BROWN: Here. It reminded me of here.

SCENE 15: *The hospital office. Present are the* DOCTOR, MATRON
and MAGGIE. *The* DOCTOR *is holding a big book—a record of
admissions, his finger on a line.*

DOCTOR: John Brown. And an address. *(To* MAGGIE) Well
done.

MAGGIE: *(troubled)* But does it make any difference?

MATRON: What was he doing round here?

DOCTOR: Staying with relatives—or holiday, we can find out.

MATRON: So long ago?

DOCTOR: Compound fracture—car accident. The driver paid
for him. . . . Well, something to go on at last!

MAGGIE: He hasn't done anything wrong, has he?

SCENE 16: BROWN's *ward. The painting nearly covers the walls.*
BROWN *is finishing it off in one corner.*

BROWN: I was a Regular, you see, and peace didn't match up
to the war I'd had. There was too much going on.

MAGGIE: So what did you do then?

BROWN: This and that. Didn't fancy a lot. *(He paints)*
Shouldn't you be working, or something?

MAGGIE: I'll go if you like.

BROWN: I like you being here. Just wondered.

MAGGIE: Wondered what?

BROWN: I'm telling you about myself, aren't I? I shouldn't
put you in that position—if they find out they'll

blame you for not passing it on.

MAGGIE: But you haven't done anything wrong, have you, Brownie?

BROWN: Is that what you're here for?

MAGGIE: No.

(BROWN *finishes off the painting and stands back*)

BROWN: There.

MAGGIE: It's lovely.

BROWN: Yes. Quite good. It'll be nice, to sit here inside my painting. I'll enjoy that.

SCENE 17: *The hospital office. The* DOCTOR *is on the phone.*

DOCTOR: . . . Brown. John Brown—yes, he was here before, a long time ago—we've got him in the records—Mmm—and an address. We'll start checking . . . there must be *somebody*. . . .

SCENE 18: BROWN's *ward. The walls are covered with paintings.* BROWN *is sitting on the bed. The door opens and a strange nurse—* NURSE JONES—*enters with* BROWN's *lunch on a tray.*

JONES: Are you ready for lunch—? *(Sees the painting)* My, my, aren't you clever.

BROWN: Where's Maggie?

JONES: Nurse Coates? I don't know.

BROWN: But—she's my nurse.

JONES: Yours? Well, she's everybody's.

BROWN: *(worried)* You don't understand—she's looking after *me*, you see.

(*The* DOCTOR *enters;* NURSE JONES *leaves*)

DOCTOR: *(cheerful)* Well, Mr. Brown—good news!

BROWN: *(wary)* Yes?

DOCTOR: You're going to have visitors.

BROWN: Visitors?

DOCTOR: Your sister Mabel and her husband. They were
            amazed to hear from you.

BROWN: They didn't hear from me.

DOCTOR: They're traveling up tomorrow. All your friends had
            been wondering where you'd got to—

BROWN: Where's Nurse Coates gone?

DOCTOR: Nowhere. She's round about. I understand that you
            were here once before—as a child.

BROWN: Yes. *(Angrily)* You couldn't leave well enough alone,
            could you?

DOCTOR: *(pause; not phoney any more)* It's not enough, Mr.
            Brown. You've got to . . . connect. . . .

SCENE 19: *The hospital office.* BROWN *appears, dressed, carrying
his bags, from the direction of his room. He sees* MAGGIE *and
stops. She sees him.*

MAGGIE: Brownie! Where are you going?

BROWN: Back.

MAGGIE: Back where? *(He does not answer)* You blame me?

BROWN: No. No. I don't *really*. You had to tell them, didn't
        you?

MAGGIE: I'm sorry—I—

BROWN: You thought it was for the best.

MAGGIE: Yes, I did. I still do. It's not good for you, what
        you're doing.

BROWN: How do you know?—*you* mean it wouldn't be good
        for *you*. How do you know what's good for me?

MAGGIE: They're coming tomorrow. Family, friends; isn't that
        good?

BROWN: I could have found them, if I'd wanted. I didn't
        come here for that. *(Comes up to her)* They won.
        (Looks out through the front doors) I feel I should
        breathe in before going out there.

MAGGIE: I can't let you go, Brownie.

BROWN: *(gently mocking)* Regulations?

MAGGIE: I can't.

BROWN: I'm free to come and go. I'm paying.

MAGGIE: I know—but it *is* a hospital.

BROWN: *(smiles briefly)* I'm not ill. Don't wake the doctor, he
        doesn't like being woken. *(Moves)* Don't be sorry—I
        had a good time here with you. Do you think they'll
        leave my painting?

MAGGIE: Brownie . . .

BROWN: Trouble is, I've always been so *well*. If I'd been *sick*
        I would have been all right.

(He goes out into the night)

Number of Words: 4596 ÷ _____ Minutes Reading Time = Rate _____

I. SUMMARY

Check √ four sentences below that could be included in a summary of the play.

_____ **1.** John Brown arrives at a hospital and wants to stay.

_____ **2.** John Brown is a very sick man.

_____ **3.** He thinks the hospital is a perfect place to live.

_____ **4.** Little by little, he tells Nurse Coates about himself, and the hospital gets in touch with his relatives.

_____ **5.** John Brown falls in love with his nurse and marries her.

_____ **6.** John Brown is alarmed by the problems befalling other people.

_____ **7.** John Brown chooses the hospital as an escape from all his worldly responsibilities.

5 points for each correct answer   SCORE: _____

II. CAUSE/EFFECT

Match each cause in column A to its effect in column B. Write the letter in the space provided.

A	B
_____ **1.** John Brown wanted to get away from the world.	**a.** Brown told her about his past.
_____ **2.** The matron didn't want him to be idle.	**b.** Brown packed his bags and left the room.
_____ **3.** Nurse Coates became Brown's friend.	**c.** She persuaded him to paint.
_____ **4.** The doctor called Brown's relatives.	**d.** He took a room in a hospital.

5 points for each correct answer   SCORE: _____

III. SUPPORTING DETAILS

Check √ five items below that John Brown told Nurse Coates about himself and his past.

_____ **1.** He had a family.

_____ **2.** He was a forger.

_____ **3.** He had been a soldier.

_____ **4.** He was married.

_____ **5.** He had been abroad.

_____ **6.** He had painted tanks.

_____ **7.** He was taken prisoner.

4 points for each correct answer   SCORE: _____

IV. VOCABULARY

Circle the letter (a, b or c) of the word or words that best give the meaning of the italicized word in each sentence.

1. The nurse was *aggrieved* at having to wake up the doctor.
   a. relieved   **b.** unhappy   **c.** angry
2. Brown admitted that he was in the hospital to *malinger*.
   a. get well   **b.** obtain work   **c.** avoid work
3. You can't just *languish* away in here.
   a. waste   **b.** work   **c.** hammer
4. Life will be nice in a *pastoral* setting.
   a. pretty   **b.** religious   **c.** peaceful

10 points for each correct answer   SCORE: _____

PERFECT TOTAL SCORE: 100   TOTAL SCORE: _____

V. QUESTION FOR THOUGHT

Do you think that John Brown should have been allowed to live the kind of life he was looking for in the hospital? Explain.